# Everyone's 2nd Chess Book

## by

## NM Dan Heisman

**Thinkers' Press, Inc.**
**Davenport Iowa**
**2000**

Everyone's 2nd Chess Book
First printing: October 2000

ISBN: 0-938650-55-6

THINKERS'
PRESS

Requests for permissions and republication rights should be addressed in writing to:

Bob Long, Editor-in-Chief
Thinkers' Press, Inc.
P.O. Box 8
Davenport, IA 52805-0008 USA
e-mail: blong@chessco.com

## Dedication

To Harvey, Holly, Cheer, Reggie, and Selma. We'll miss you. And to Shelly, who somehow puts up with her husband's long hours at the computer—not always writing chess books!

# CONTENTS

# Introduction

*Everyone's 2nd Chess Book* is my third chess book. I like to think this one, like the others, is unique, helpful, and contributes to the world of chess knowledge.

Almost all beginner's chess books are written with one of two ideas in mind:

1. Teach the student the basic rules, like checkmate, how the pieces move, and a few basic principles, or
2. Provide a series of basic tactical exercises (pins, forks, double attacks, etc.) to help the beginner learn to spot simple combinations and then help him progress to more complex winning exercises.

However, based upon my chess teaching experiences with hundreds of beginners, young and old, there is a definite gap between the time you learn the rules and the point at which doing tactical problems is feasible. This gap consists of the period when the beginner's brain learns to recognize more easily the possible moves that each piece can make, both by the beginner's pieces and his opponents', as well as understanding the value of pieces and figuring out when each piece is safe. *Everyone's 2nd Chess Book* is designed to fill the gap between "How to Play" books and "Beginning Tactics" books–the missing link.

Not many of these beginner's books attempt to cover the mental process that a beginner goes through during this gap. *Everyone's 2nd Chess Book* covers quite a bit of this process by discussing the general term **"board vision,"** which has to do with how the brain, through memory, visual input, and pattern recognition, grows to understand what is happening on a chess board.

The problem with the approach in beginning tactics books is that at first beginners lack the board vision to remember and use the knowledge from the exercises. They need some experience between the time they learn the basic moves until the time they are able to consistently solve simple tactical exercises. For example, most beginners need time and experience just to recognize when their pieces are safe and how to count whether they come out ahead, behind, or even through exchanges. Almost all beginners need to master this step before they can learn how to win a piece through a pin.

Just as GM Andrew Soltis addressed serious players in his *The Catalog of Chess Mistakes,* this book provides the many "What to Avoids" for beginning chess players. In addition, it provides a series of "Improvement Tips" that will help all beginning chess students improve their game at a rapid rate.

### IMAGES

Many years ago Grandmaster Nikolai Krogius wrote a book called *Chess Psychology.* But unlike other books on chess psychology, he wrote not only about "psyching out" your opponent or "playing like a tiger," but instead categorizing areas of psychological mistakes related to what I am calling board vision. Krogius defined:

- *the retained image*–when analyzing a position you accidentally visualize leaving a piece where it was instead of realizing it was moved during the intended combination
- *the inert image*–in unbalanced (especially winning) positions, the inability to suddenly switch the focus to a dynamically new counterchance of your opponent
- *the advance image*–the imagined threats of a player's opponent become so strong that the player loses all objectivity in trying to deal with the perceived, but not necessarily actual threat.

All of the above are primarily characteristics of *advanced play.* Watching beginners play, I have found conclusively that the reason newcomers leave pieces *en prise* (French for: able to be captured) or miss simple tactics is *not* necessarily because of their lack of knowledge (of tactics, for example), but just because they lack the necessary board vision to "see" which of their opponent's pieces are attacking a square or that any tactic at all is possible.

Teaching a tactic to a beginner before they develop the necessary board vision produces diminishing returns, because the knowledge to use the tactic is hampered by the inability to see that the pieces involved are set up for the tactic. Until I understood this, I found it frustrating to show beginners basic pins and forks, only to see them completely miss these same tactics immediately thereafter during their games. Once I understood why, I began to concentrate on helping beginners develop better board vision as quickly as possible. *After the beginner gained the necessary board vision capabilities, then* they picked up tactics much more readily, as they could "see" what was happening when it occurred in their games.

This book deals with a broad range of "board vision" problems, concentrating mainly on those that occur during the *beginner and intermediate* levels—I think Krogius and others have done a fine job explaining what happens on the advanced level. Therefore, besides *Everyone's 2nd Chess Book* or *Chess Vision: You Can't Play What You Don't See*, we could also have named this book, *Developing Board Vision, Beginning Chess Psychology, Chess Thinking Development*, or even *Beginner's Chess Mistakes*. No matter what the name, we will be examining the problems and mistakes chessplayers run into during the early stages of their chess development.

We will also cover some other important bits of information about rules, etiquette, etc. that pertain to the early period of chess development. Any helpful topic is fair prey, especially if it aids beginning players. The idea of the book is therefore to not only cover how one advances after learning how to make the moves, but also to provide practical advice both for players at this level as well as for those who may be instructing them. We only assume that the reader knows what is in the most basic beginner's books: how to move the pieces, the basic rules regarding checkmate and draws, and algebraic notation.

*Everyone's 2nd Chess Book* is primarily aimed at the following readership:

- Chess Instructors
- Scholastic Chess Sponsors
- Interested Parents
- Beginning Chess Players Teenage Level and Above
- Anyone interested in how beginners learn to play (better) chess

## CLOSE TO HOME

*Everyone's 2nd Chess Book* covers the lower to medium level student, with USCF ratings below 1400—and for the most part, below 1000. (Note: ratings range from 0 to about 2800, which is world champion level.) These are the vast majority of players, and the ones who make the kind of serious mistakes we will try to teach you to avoid.

Thanks in part to the movie, *Searching for Bobby Fischer*, the need for this book has soared. The U.S. Chess Federation (USCF) reports that the number of junior memberships has gone from about 5,000 in 1990 to over 40,000 by 1998. Correspondingly, the median rating of USCF players has dropped from about 1500 to about 1100 as more youthful, beginning players enter the wonderful world of tournament play.

If you are wondering just how familiar I, a battle-scarred master, am with this lower level of play, consider the following:

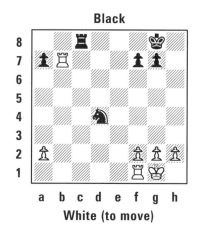

**Black**

**White (to move)**

"Delen is setting himself up to be checkmated."

I was talking to one of my best students, James. James was 11 at the time and his rating was almost 1800. We were at the *1996 World Open* in Philadelphia. The player with the white pieces was **my son**, Delen, one of the favorites though in the always unpredictable Under 1000 Section.

James smiled in disbelief because, unlike myself, he hadn't seen Delen commit self-mate countless times. Delen is a smart kid and, at age 13, had been playing tournament chess for 6 years. But just the fact that Delen was still in the Under 1000 Section is enough to tell you that he plays just for fun, and is not at all that interested in improving.

## 1. Rxa7

Delen plays the correct move, but I know from his previous pattern that it is a sign of trouble. One of my primary guidelines for my students is:

**When you are winning you should think defense first. You don't have to win "more;" you should make sure you won't lose.**

## 1. ... Rd8!

Now I really started to worry. Even though Black was a much weaker player than my son, he was setting up a couple of traps that would surely win the game if Delen wasn't alert.

## 2. Re1?

Again, not really a bad move, but indicative of the wrong frame of mind.

What *should* White be thinking? He is up the Exchange and two pawns, so if he removes all of Black's threats he would probably win. Therefore, in practice the best move for a player like Delen would be 2. h3!, removing all back rank threats. At least Delen did not fall for the superficial "good" pin with 2. Rd1? when 2...Ne2† 3. Kf1 (Delen might even play 3. Kh1??? allowing 3...Rxd1#) Rxd1† 4. Kxe2 would still win, although not nearly as easily.

## 2. ... Ne2†!

Black really has nothing to lose by playing this trap. I had taught Delen to write his move down first before making it, put his pencil over the move, make a sanity check of the board, and then, only if this check passes, finally touch his piece. Some of this Delen did, but unfortunately his entire process took about 3 seconds! This short time even included the sanity check, which consisted of just seeing if the Knight was really unguarded.

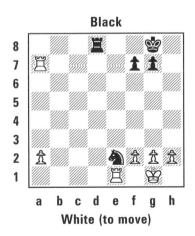

**Black**

**White (to move)**

## 3. Rxe2?? Rd1†

Well, it was not mate, but Delen's opponent said so and Delen resigned, as mate comes next move.

James looked at me, trying not

to smile. Delen wasn't too upset, but as usual his Master dad
was trying to avoid apoplexy. If
I die of a heart attack before you
read this, now you will know why.

**At Play. Notice the "itchy" finger.**

# 1: Learning, Chunking, and Chess Mistakes

When humans learn a complex subject, such as reading or chess, they learn in "chunks." These chunks of information gradually get more complex, corresponding to the level of information the learner is currently able to process. For example, when a child learns to read, the levels representing these chunks are something like:

1. Recognizing which shapes are which letters
2. Remembering which letter makes which sound
3. Putting letters together to make multiple sounds, such as words
4. Recognizing words (and their meanings–although this is usually already known from learning how to talk)
5. Scanning several words, a line, or even multiple lines for content

**Chess' Complexity**

~ 13 ~

There is a reading trick you may have seen. One puts the word "the" in a sentence twice consecutively, once at the end of a line and once at the start of the next. You then ask someone to read the sentence, which you place in the middle of a paragraph. Most of the time an experienced reader will not read both "the's." It is the reader's chunking capability at reading "level 5" that makes this trick work.

When your reading chunks are at a higher level (adults are almost all at level 5), then you can read quite a bit faster, but you no longer notice the individual words and letters in the same way you did when you were at a lower level. However, a beginning reader at level 3 or 4 will be processing a word at a time and will almost always see the two "thes."

Learning how to play chess can be thought of in exactly the same way. As one progresses in chess, he will go through similar "levels":

1. Recognizing pieces
2. Remembering how pieces move
3. Determining legal moves for each piece
4. Determining reasonable moves for each piece

5. Seeing the whole board and determining reasonable plans for your entire set of pieces

## Board Vision

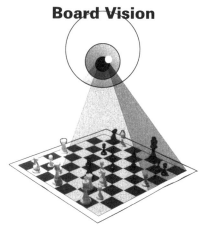

I consider these chunking levels to be classified as "board vision" capabilities because each is a cognitive problem the brain must recognize through its visual input. Thus, each player looking at the board sees different things based upon his level, just as a non-football fan would not be able to recognize a blitzing linebacker when watching a game–instead he might ask "what is a linebacker?"

The following provides an example of how a player at each level might think if he had Paul Morphy's position in this famous game:

**Duke of Brunswick
and Count Isouard**

**Morphy**

Level 1: "Is that my Queen or my King here close to me?"

Level 2: "Let's see, my Knight moves like an 'L.' "

Level 3: "Can that white Rook jump over the black Knight?"

Level 4: "If I move my Queen up and check on b8, he can take me with his Knight."

Level 5: "His back rank looks vulnerable to a mating attack. Can I clear the Knight out of the way? Yes! After a Queen check on b8 my Rook can mate on d8."

These attributes of board vision also explains why I could not play blindfold chess when I started, but could later; it is impossible to play blindfolded before you reach level 5, but not so difficult for many level 5 players (though of course they would differ greatly in playing strength,

just as they do when they are looking!).

An adult who is not a serious player but plays chess with his friends easily gets to level 4 but may never get to level 5, while a child playing tournament chess (very) seriously can reach level 5 at a fairly young age, say eight or nine.

Translating chunking capabilities into USCF ratings (note: the higher the rating the better. Garry Kasparov, Bobby Fischer, and Deep Blue are all about 2800; master level starts at 2200, and no one can have a rating below 0!), here are common board vision problems for lower rated players:

**Under 100 (Level 1):** Does not yet recognize all the pieces all the time.

**100-200 (Level 2):** Recognizes the pieces, but has trouble remembering how each piece moves.

**200-400 (Level 3):** Has trouble recognizing what the pieces can do, especially with regard to legality, such as moving into check or looking for illegal moves. During a game between two players at this level the board positions tend to be somewhat random. Players often move very fast and "see" almost none of the possibilities; i.e., board vision tends to be almost non-existent.

**400-600 (Low Level 4):** Focuses almost exclusively on his own pieces; usually doesn't consider opponent's possibilities. Therefore often puts pieces in take *(en prise)* and still makes and allows illegal moves occasionally. Tends to move very fast.

**600-800 (Intermediate Level 4):** Can chunk some of the board, but doesn't look for alternative moves; still has trouble taking into account the opponent's moves. Still puts pieces *in take.* Almost all of the game is legal. Tends to move relatively quickly without thinking of consequences of their move or opponent's previous move.

**800-1000 (Upper Level 4):** Able to "see" the board but sometimes misses pieces on the perimeter (such as a far-away Bishop); can make some plans but has no idea what is important in the position. Misses simple mates for both sides and still may put pieces *in take* occasionally. Still marked by Level 4 understanding; i.e., sees primarily parts of the board and piece moves, but doesn't chunk as much of the position as a Level 5 player would.

**1000-1200 (Hazy area between Level 4 and Level 5):** For the most part no longer puts pieces in take, but still has difficulty seeing and avoiding simple combinations. Has a tendency to come up with unnecessarily complex solutions to simple problems. Is able to see ahead on the board but still has difficulty understanding what is important in the position.

**1200-1400 (Level 5):** The beginning of higher level chess. Players no longer just win because one just gave away more pieces than the other. Level 5 chunking is now becoming apparent in a player's analysis.

Even adult players who are able to achieve Level 5 chunking may make enormous board vision errors when confronted with an unusual situation. At the 1970 Interzonal at Palma de Mallorca, during a tense endgame with both a *pin* and a *pawn lever* causing difficult tactics, a tired Efim Geller, hallucinated against Bobby Fischer and made a famous mistake by thinking his King was pinning a pawn to a Rook!

**Sudden Death Time Controls**

On a much more humorous level, two adults in the 1200-1500 range made the following board vision error:

This unusual four-Queen position was reached during a club game, and both players had less than five minutes left to complete the *sudden death time control* (i.e., they had to make all their moves in this remaining time). As the Tournament Director, I had retrieved two Queens from another set for the second pair of Queens (they were not playing with upside-down Rooks). The second, borrowed "pair" were the Queens on b7 and f3. The lack of board vision for unusual positions, even for relatively experienced adults, began to show as Black played the terrible ...Qd3†???, putting his original Queen *in take*. White hesitated, but played the obvious and correct Qxd3.

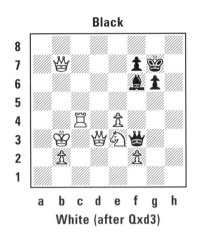

White (after Qxd3)

At this point *much* stranger things began to happen. White decided it might be a good idea if the player owning the other two Queens got those two pieces back. White therefore first picked up his capturing white Queen, the original one *still on the board at d3*, and replaced the borrowed Queen on b7 (*never putting back anything on d3!!*), and then took the captured black Queen (the original one that was now *off* the board) and used it to replace the borrowed Queen on f3, creating the following position (with only the set's original Queens on the board) without any "chess" moves being made!!

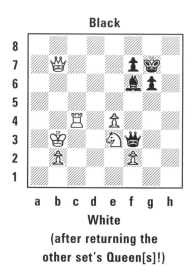

**Black**

White

(after returning the
other set's Queen[s]!)

Yes, White has literally "Given away a Queen"–the extra one with which he had captured on d3!!! **Neither player noticed what had happened until I told them after the game!** How is it possible that experienced adult players could make such a mistake?

Part from my discussion with the participants, I contend that it was because of the following factors:

1. Both players were in time trouble and, under pressure, were not thinking clearly.
2. The position was unusual, as both players had been playing with two Queens. If the position had been with one Queen each, then White would have certainly noticed if he had given his only Queen away. But since they were in a very rare position where he had two Queens to one, it was much easier to "normalize" the position back to one Queen each, as if the extra Queens had been traded.
3. The two extra Queens had only been on the board for a few moves (which in real time, had only been a minute or two), so it was easier for White to miss the fact that the position had changed drastically and he was now up a Queen! I don't think this would have happened if the players had been rated closer to 2000.

Returning to chess development, there is another aspect that should be mentioned, and that is the issue of age and brain development. For example, almost all players below age 8 have a difficult time "caring" about their opponent's moves. They have fun moving their pieces as a type of "problem solving" but no interest in the other player or solving problems their opponent poses to them. This seems to be directly correlated with personal development away from chess, as the youthful ego is strong, but the perception of other's feelings (empathy) has not yet been well developed. As players get older and better, they begin to realize that it is equally as important to solve the problems the opponent is making for them as it is to pose problems for that opponent.

Most chess books are written for either absolute beginners (Getting you quickly from Levels 1 through Level 3) or experienced players looking to get better (Low to high Level 5). Unfortunately, most chess-playing children are either at Level 4 or do not yet have the intellectual development to fully operate at Level 5. In addition, as was a central theme in my book, *Elements of Positional Evaluation*, many players are incorrectly taught stringent "rules" that should just be learned as helpful "guidelines," and thus continue to make the kind of mistakes we will discuss in later chapters.

Therefore, there is somewhat of a gap in chess literature. We will address some of the most common kid's mistakes, especially at Level 4. We will try to examine why the mistake occurred and what general thinking guidelines would help you (or someone you are teaching) avoid making a similar mistake.

# The Eleven Most Common Mistakes of Players Rated 800-1400

800-1400 is the USCF rating of most of my students when they begin lessons. I see students in this range make the same mistakes over and over again. The following is a "Top-10" List of the most common mistakes – almost all of them either related to board vision or inexperience:

## 1. Missing A Simple Tactic

Since being tactically sound is the main prerequisite for becoming an intermediate player, it follows that all beginners need to improve on their tactics. Not just combinations, but even simple motifs such as the most basic, counting (i.e., determining when a series of captures gains or loses material), as well as the standards such as pins, double attacks, x-rays, forks, removal of the guard, overworked piece, interference, etc.

## 2. Not Looking at What Your Opponent is Threatening

Beginners, especially youngsters, have a tendency to be "overwhelmed" (or preoccupied) with their own possibilities. Often the opponent makes an easy threat and a simple "What can he do to me now that he couldn't do to me before?" would suffice. Discovered or far-ranging threats from the fast moving pieces (Bishops, Rooks, and Queens) are easily missed.

### 3. Not Getting All Pieces Into Play

Of all the problems on the list, this is the most perplexing. Often I have very bright, mature students, who simply cannot follow the guideline, "Always get ALL of your pieces into the game." I guess they are seduced by the forces of the "Dark Side." A couple of years ago John Keir, a parent of one of my students, was playing in his second tournament. He easily swept aside all six opponents in his Under 1200 section, taking home some nice first place money. I immediately asked him how he did it. "Simple," John said, "All I did was pay attention when you were giving my son lessons about how important it was to get all your pieces in the game and I did. My opponents did not and I just got a good game and won!" If only I could bottle this attitude and sell it. Unfortunately most of my younger students want to do something as soon as possible and don't have the patience to wait until all their forces are ready.

### 4. Not Knowing Basic Opening Traps

It is unfortunate, but playing good chess requires not just skill but also knowledge. Even beginners need to be schooled on some of the most basic traps in the open-

ings they play. One player from our club, who has never taken any lessons or read any books but has a world of talent, lost in the opening after getting a bad position out of the Black side of the Fried Liver Attack, of which he knew nothing. Just a couple of hours of going over his basic opening moves would have allowed him to survive.

### 5. Phantom Fears

While a common error, this one is not so easy to correct for the improving player. This problem entails a kind of "lazy thinking" whereby the beginner does not

## The 11 Most Common Mistakes of Players Rated 800-1400

1 Missing a simple tactic
2 Not looking at what your opponent is threatening
3 Not getting all pieces into play
4 Not knowing basic opening traps
5 Phantom fears
6 Overly worried about the value of the pieces
7 Overly worried about positional liabilities
8 Playing too fast
9 Not looking for a better move
10 Being afraid of the opponent
11 Worrying about your rating

actually analyze to see if a continuation is possible, but rather assumes the opponent can or might do something harmful. Unfortunately, this assumption is often faulty, and the beginner often bypasses the correct continuation out of fear of something totally impossible or easily preventable.

### 6. Overly Worried About the Value of the Pieces

I call this one of the "Reinfeld" problems, and it is becoming more widely recognized. The problem is that giving the pieces values is a such a valuable and necessary "principle" to beginners that they often don't get the follow-up: these values are not absolute! Play the position. For example, everyone understands that in the endgame it is better to have only one pawn left than to have one Knight because Knights can't mate. But a pawn can become a Queen that does mate! Unfortunately many are unable to carry over this concept in general—that material is relative and in some positions a fianchettoed Bishop or Outpost Knight may be doing a lot more than a Rook stuck behind closed lines.

## 7. Overly Worried About Positional Liabilities

I call this the "I don't want to win the Queen because then my pawns are doubled" problem. Beginners need to understand that positional considerations are great tiebreaks when the material is even, but once one side is up a piece or more, considerations like trading off your opponents attacking material almost always is much more important than whether you get doubled pawns in the process.

## 8. Playing Too Fast

It took my son a period of regular tournament play before he realized that he might actually see a little more, and be a little more careful if he took his time. I always say, "The Powers That Be gave you the talent and the Tournament Director gave you the time, so use both to the maximum extent possible!" Board vision and

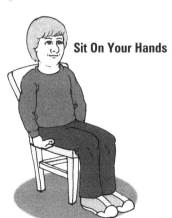

**Sit On Your Hands**

the use of time go hand in hand, so the next chapter will deal with this interesting topic.

**Some tips for slowing down (see the next chapter for more detailed information):**

- Sit on your hands so you don't move as soon as your opponent does.
- If you see a good move, look for a better one
- Realize your brains are not in your fingers
- Playing fast almost always helps your opponent
- All the good players play at least somewhat slow, and there is good reason for this

## 9. Not Looking for a Better Move

As mentioned above, "If you see a good move, look for a better one!" Beginners are sometimes so overjoyed that their move looks good that they don't realize sometimes there are much better ones around. Recently my son saw that he could take a pawn with check, so he did so in a split second. Unfortunately the check lost by force. Instead, he could have played a mate in one if he had just looked for a few seconds.

## 10. Being Afraid of the Opponent

I often hear from players rated X, "Uh-oh, I am playing someone rated X+200. I am sure to lose." This is bad "thinking" for several reasons:

• According to the rating system, even if the ratings were perfectly accurate, you will still win 24% of the games from someone rated 200 points higher.

• If you think you will lose, you probably will, since chess is a mental sport and thinking you will lose hurts your mental attitude.

• As a Master, I have to admit it sounds a little silly when an 1100 player tells me how good a 1300 player is. After all, if 1300 is so good, how come the average experienced tournament player is rated well above that, and a 1300 rating is near the bottom of the USCF's Top-50 list for 9-10 year olds! It is just a relative state of mind that a beginner has to overcome. I say that:

**When you lose your fear of players with a certain rating, only then can you become that rating.**

## BONUS MISTAKE #11

## 11. Worrying about your rating.

Ratings are fun and helpful, but they just follow your playing strength.

**In the long run your rating does not go up or down because of any particular set of wins and losses, but because you got worse or, hopefully, better. If you want your rating to go up, don't worry about losing, worry about learning.**

And, paradoxically, if you are one of those who can learn by their mistakes and not repeat them (too much), then by losing you will learn more and, in the long run, get a higher rating. That is why I advise my students to play opponents, human and computer, that are about 200 rating points above them—just enough to push them and not enough to discourage them.

## Losing

In the above discussion, we touched upon the fear of losing. An understanding of losing and how it affects a player is a subject worthy of an entire book. However, although this is not that book, losing has such a strong affect on beginners (and is so misunderstood by them) that *Everyone's 2nd Chess Book* would not be complete unless we addressed the subject in at least some detail.

There is a spectrum of how a player is affected by losing, from "It doesn't bother me at all" to "I hate losing; I don't want to play because I might lose." Players at either end of the spectrum don't advance very far in chess. Those who don't care at all about losing are usually doomed to repeat their mistakes over and over again, because they don't have any motivation to find out what they did wrong and to correct it. Those who are traumatized by losing (it is too much of a blow to their ego) become paralyzed by the prospect of playing, and thus eventually stop. The stories of three players illustrate these concepts:

My son doesn't let much bother him, including losing. Therefore he has been back rank mated (as shown in the Introduction) about 20 times—many in otherwise winning positions—before he finally outgrew it. Losing in winning positions wasn't painful enough to motivate him to do the work to check and make sure there was no mate. Of course, his father will live a few years less because of this.

Another one of my college-age friends got to the expert level, but hated to lose. One time he lost a game at our local club and sat on the window sill, beet red, for over an hour, refusing to answer any questions. He soon thereafter quit chess forever.

The third player's case was more curious. He was the brightest in his high-school class. However, there were many other fine chessplayers in his school, and they were all more experienced than he was. His friends, however, did not understand the great amount of time it takes to absorb the knowledge needed to improve. They said to him, "How can you be the smartest kid in the school and not even play higher than fifth board on the chess team?" This drove him to distraction, and he couldn't bear the burden of not being the best right away. He also gave up the Royal Game.

All the best chess players fall somewhere in between the two extremes, slightly toward the "I hate to lose" side. They need to hate to lose just enough to be driven to learn how to avoid repeating their mistakes–no matter what the level of competition. But they cannot hate to lose so much that they will not study and learn from their losses.

You should look at losing not as a loss of ego, but as a learning experience. If every time you lose, you learn the cause of the loss and make a positive correction for the future, you will soon be a good player. You usually learn more from losing than from winning. This is because losing always involves a mistake of the magnitude worth noting, and also because the opponents you lose to are, usually superior to the ones you beat, and thus are better able to demonstrate something worth learning.

It is worth repeating: **you learn more when you lose, and getting better involves knowing more.** Therefore those that play stronger players enough to lose often, and are willing to learn from their losses (write down your games and go over them with your instructor!...) will get better the fastest. I always tell my beginning classes that I have undoubtedly lost more games than all of them put together...!

So next time your instructor is going over your game and tells you "that is a bad move," don't take it personally! He is trying to point out to you the kinds of mistakes you are making so you will recognize them and, hopefully, not repeat them whenever a similar situation arises.

Fear of losing can also cause students to ask for or agree to premature *draws*.

What makes you a better player is more knowledge (your innate ability is always the same!). Many students feel that drawing, especially with a higher rated player, will raise their rating. While this is true, it is also rather shortsighted and superficial. What really raises your rating *in the long run* is becoming a better player, having a higher playing strength. More knowledge will raise your playing strength and, your rating will tend to move toward your playing strength. Therefore, losing a long endgame and learning something is eventually better for your rating than agreeing to a draw at the start of the endgame due to fear of losing! The realization of this truth is an important part of becoming a good player. *I tell my students to think of early draw offers by their opponent as "Offers to stay ignorant."* None of the

**These students are paying attention, are yours?**

world's best players got their high playing strength by quickly agreeing to draws when they were learning. Bobby Fischer used to turn down draws almost without considering the position!

One of my students played a game where he agreed to a draw at the start of the endgame even though he was definitely not losing. When I asked him why he agreed to the draw, he said that he doesn't play the endgame very well, so he took the draw! I said, "Hmmm, let me see. You don't play the endgame very well, so you avoid the endgame. Does that make any sense? How are you going to improve your endgame if you try to avoid it whenever possible?"

To summarize, if you want to improve you should:

1. Learn more about chess through professional instructors, books, videos, computers, etc. ("theory"),
2. Play as much as possible, both in number of games *and in number of moves* ("practice"), and
3. Learn from your mistakes. Record your games and go over them with a strong player to identify your mistakes so that you have less chance of repeating them. For non-beginners, enter the game into a computer using the analysis mode of a strong chess program; this is the best way to spot more advanced tactical mistakes. ("feedback")

Often the best chessplayers are *not* the ones who initially make the fewest mistakes, but the ones who are able to improve by not repeating their mistakes (or at least repeating them less often)!

# 2: Developing Board Vision

## 2.1 Developing Board Vision to Reinforce Where the Pieces Can Move

There is no doubt–almost all good players initially developed their board vision by playing hundreds and thousands of chess games. But that doesn't mean that playing is the most efficient way to develop board vision; it just means that most players were never exposed to any other method. In fact, even talented beginners are at first overwhelmed by the initial setup of the pieces and need quite a bit of playing time before they can readily "see" where all the pieces can move. For this reason many chess teachers believe starting with some simple endgame positions is easier for a beginner to comprehend.

It is possible to take this line of reasoning one step further and aid development of "piece movement" board vision through a set of board vision "exercises" which focus on one (or a few) pieces at a time. Steve Shutt, of the famous Masterman (Philadelphia) High School chess program, suggested some exercises to me and, using his ideas, I developed a few of my own. The following are some examples:

**1) Pawn-taking:**The student starts with one piece on any square (it is probably a good idea to do this exercise with each piece, in the order of increasing difficulty of piece movement: Rook, then Bishop, King, Queen, and lastly, Knight). The tutor then puts a pawn of the opposite color on the board (e.g., if the student has a white Rook the tutor places black pawns). If the student can take the pawn with the piece, he does so and quickly returns the captured pawn to the tutor; if he cannot capture the pawn, he just waits. The tutor continues to put pawns on the board one at a time. When multiple pawns are on the board and one is taken, the student may continue to take more pawns so long as he can do so with only one additional piece move (in other words, if taking another pawn would require more than one additional move, he may *not* do so). The tutor should place some pawns where they can be taken and some where they cannot be taken. The exercise should continue until the student gets a "feel" for how the practice piece moves.

**2) Pawn-taking with obstacles:** In this variation of #1 the student gets a specified number of consecutive moves to capture one pawn of the opposite color. The catch is that he may not move through or to certain squares where the tutor has placed "obstruction" pawns of the color of the student's piece. An example will illustrate this clearly: The tutor puts a black pawn on an empty board along with a white Rook which cannot capture the pawn in one move. There are always two ways the

student can capture the pawn in two moves:

**The Rook can capture the pawn two moves via f6 or b3**

After the student successfully captures the pawns via one of the two routes f6-b6 or b3-b6, let's say f6-b6, then the tutor places a pawn somewhere on the f6-b6 path (e.g, on f5) so that the Rook can no longer successfully use that path to capture the pawn in two moves.

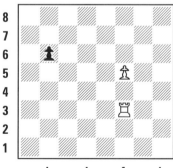

**The Rook can only capture the pawn in two moves via b3**

Once the student has found the

only remaining path to capture the pawn in two moves: b3-b6, a second white pawn is placed on the board on that path (e.g., on c3) so that now both two-move paths are blocked and it requires three moves to capture the pawn on b6.

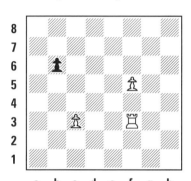

**The Rook needs three moves to capture the pawn—all legal first moves are possible**

As the student continues to find paths to capture the pawn in three moves, these paths are also blocked by the tutor with a pawn:

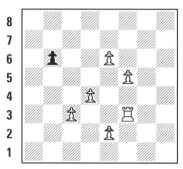

**In the final position the Rook can only capture the pawn in three moves via f1**

This exercise continues with a piece until the student learns to successfully look for multiple ways that a piece can reach a destination. This exercise thus helps develop not only board vision, but also look-ahead and planning skills.

**3) Ruler force fields:** In this exercise the student puts a Rook, Bishop, or Queen on the Board. He then uses one or more rulers to show the lines of force "emanating" from the piece. For Knights and Kings, the student should put pawns on the board representing all the legal moves of the piece.

**4) Knight "Tours"**–There are many variations on this theme. The simplest one is to have the student put a Knight on the board and have the tutor point to a square. The student then tries to move the Knight to that square with the minimum number of moves (or as quickly) as possible. In a second variation the Knight must find its way from one corner to another. These tasks can be made more difficult by placing pawns (obstacles) on the board which make the squares they are on inaccessible. For more advanced students, the task can be made harder still by extending this rule so that not only are the squares the pawns are on inaccessible, but so are the *squares the pawns attack*! (This latter exercise is exemplified by the "Chess IQ" test, which I first saw when it was published over 30 years ago in *Chess Life*:)

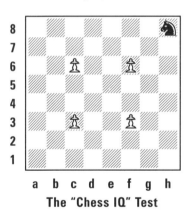

The "Chess IQ" Test

The student must find legal Knight moves to go, in order, from h8 to g8 to f8 to … a8 to a7 to c7 to f7 to h7 to h6 …zig-zagging left then right and then back again until reaching all of the squares along the first rank (h1 is the final square). The student must avoid moving to any squares where the white pawns reside *as well as the ones they attack*. In other words, b7, d7, e7, g7, c6, f6, etc. can never be landed upon during the entire exercise–they are neither target squares nor can be used to get to target squares! The test is timed.

The original article said that once a student has a modicum of board vision, this exercise can be used to test aptitude "independent" of chess knowledge. The student is supposed to take the test twice, one trial right after another. The tutor adds a penalty for each illegal move (10 seconds). The speed of the first test measures raw aptitude and the gain in time for the second try measures learning ability. Supposedly a first attempt taking five minutes or less shows International Master potential, while three minutes or less shows Grandmaster potential. Since I started playing serious chess at 16, I knew I never was going to become a Grandmaster, but that is another story (see my second book, *The Improving Annotator: From Beginner to Master*).

**5) Dan's Special Knight Obstacle Course:** This is for those who like mazes. I place a Knight and a King of the *opposite color* on the board in any position except a Knight's move apart. I then add many obstacles in the form of all the other pieces (their color doesn't matter–only the Knight and the opposite color King). The Knight has to make as many consecutive Knight moves as it takes to "capture" the King. The following are some (increasingly harder) example "Obstacle Courses" with the white Knight trying to capture the black King and the white pawns as obstacles:

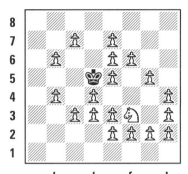

C. This slightly harder maze also has many solutions: e.g., Nd2-e4-g3-h5-f4-xd5

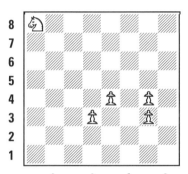

A. This maze for beginners requires care to get to f2, e.g.: Nb6-a4-b2-f2-xh1

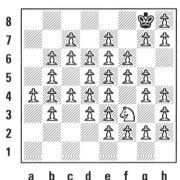

D. White must do something like: Nd2-f1-g3-h5-f4-g6-f8-d7-b8-a6-c5-b7-d8-f7-h6-xg8!

(To make the above easier, remove the pawn on b4 or the one at h8! When finished go to the diagram on the next page.)

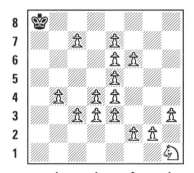

B. This easy maze has many solutions, e.g.: Ng3-f5-d6-c4-b6-xa8

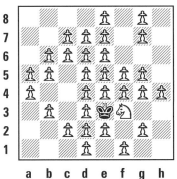

E. Try Ng1-h3-f2-h1-g3-
h5-f6-h7-f8-g6-h8-f7-d8-b7-
c5-a6-b4-a2-c3-b1-a3-c4-xe3!

The above exercises can be done with other pieces, such as Rooks and Bishops, although the Knight is the most "fun."

## 2.2 Developing Checkmate Vision

There is a difference between recognizing (statically) what is a checkmate and learning how to give (dynamically) a simple (Q, Q&R, 2 Q's, 2 R's, R) checkmate.

After teaching hundreds of elementary school children who initially didn't know how to move the pieces (as part of the inner city Chess in Schools' *Get Smart* program), I found that understanding the concept of checkmate was much harder than, say, learning to name all the squares.

One of the problems is that checkmate is abstract–you never take off a King; you just have to prove that you could do it on the next move. It is somewhat like teaching children the difference between a *capture* and an *attack;* with a capture you take off a piece permanently, while with an "attack" you merely threaten to do so *next move.* **Check** is just an attack on a King, while **checkmate** indicates that the threat cannot be parried and that there is no legal move to get out of check. One has to explain that the rules do not allow some plausible defenses–such as counterattacking the opponent's King or even attacking (*but not capturing!*) the piece that is checking the King. In checkers, it is all much simpler–take off all the opponent's pieces and you win. In *Monopoly,* get everyone else's money. But in chess if your opponent moves his King into check, you not only cannot win by taking it off the board, you must "help" your opponent by telling him that the move is illegal and having him make a legal one. Many a game seems to have been won by students who declared "I won. I took off his King..."

Therefore, Steve Shutt's suggestion to teach checkmate by example makes sense. Using an extension of the "Ruler Force Field" exercise, he uses the Two-

An extension of the
"Ruler Force Field"
exercise (see pg. 29)

Rook mate whereby the Rooks force the King up the board:

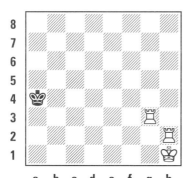

Defining mate by example:
The "force fields" emanate
out of the left side of the Rooks
as the King is forced
"upward": 1. Rh4†

2. Rg5†

1... Kb5

2... Kc6

3. Rh6†

3... Kd7

4. Rg7†

4... Ke8

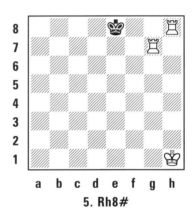

5. Rh8#

## Defining Checkmate

One unfortunate drawback to showing mate by an example is that the concept of "definition" vs. "example" is not always clear in a fourth-grader's head. Even though I go to great pains to explain that **checkmate is when an attacked King cannot get out of check,** after showing the two-Rook example I often get fed back the "definition:" "Checkmate is when the Rook is attacking the

King and the King can't move…"! When I explain again that this was an example but not the definition of checkmate, I still get 2nd tries that start "Checkmate is when a Rook…"

Once the concept of checkmate has been established, there are two basic things to be learned:

1) Patterns of what is and isn't checkmate, and

2) How to force checkmate in the most common, simple cases (with just a Q, Q+R, 2 Q's, 2 R's, or just a R).

Visual aids can be used to illustrate multiple checkmate possibilities. For example, if the white King is placed on f2, a white Queen on g4, and a black King on h1, the student is asked to find all the squares where the white Queen can successfully checkmate the black King. A white pawn can be placed on a square for a successful guess and a black pawn on a square for an unsuccessful guess (I sometimes put the pawns on the board lying sideways so that the student doesn't get confused and start to think there are actually pawns in the way!). After seven guesses (five successful), the board might look something like this:

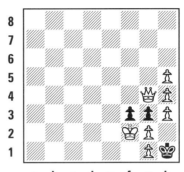

Pawns indicate successful and unsuccessful mate-in-1 guesses

There are many ways to show checkmate patterns and many good books on the subject. Laszlo Polgar, father of the famous Polgar sisters, published a book of his problems which starts out with over 300 Mate-in-ones! These examples help establish checkmate patterns and how to force it in one-move settings, but do not directly address what is *not* checkmate (except by the student's failed attempts…). Other books have problems sets of the type: "Which of the following positions is checkmate?," which directly focuses on this question. I think these type of problems are more beneficial *before* going the Polgar approach.

## 2.3 Developing the Ability to Count Material on Potential Exchanges

Tactical problems are designed to help the beginner learn to recognize combinations that either win material or checkmate. However, as mentioned in the Introduction, a beginner is unable to do these tactical exercises until they recognize two more basic principles:

1) when a piece is being attacked and can be taken for free, and

2) evaluating potential exchanges to determine if they come out ahead, behind, or even (I call an exchange that comes out even "a fair trade").

The ability to calculate whether or not an exchange is favorable is necessary for the important ability to figure out whether a given piece is safe. This is especially true when the piece is on a square both attacked by some of the opponent's pieces and guarded by some of a player's other pieces.

Pieces that can be taken for free are called *"en prise* (pron.: on pree)." The exercises earlier in this chapter will help any beginner learn to recognize when either their or their opponent's pieces are *en prise*. However, the most important part of learning to recognize when pieces are *en prise* is learning to take your time and look around (See Chapter 6, *Board Vision and Time*).

However, there are exercises that can enhance a beginner's ability to see whether or not an exchange is favorable. I will present a few of these here, and any instructor will be able to set up some more, once they see the idea. I call these "Counting" exercises. In the next chapter, we include a guideline on the values of the pieces:

*As a ROUGH guide, consider Knights and Bishops as worth about 3 Pawns* (not 3 points!), *Rooks 5 Pawns, and Queens 9. Pawns, of course, are worth 1.* We will use these values in the counting exercises.

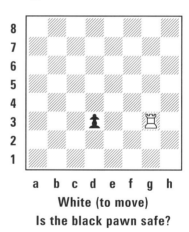

**White (to move)**
**Is the black pawn safe?**

The answer, of course, is "No." 1. Rxd3 would win the pawn. Too easy, you say? OK, let us build up the difficulty one step at a time.

Since you have the pawn attacked once and it is guarded zero times, you can win it.

White (to move)

**Is the black pawn safe?**

Now the answer is "Yes." After 1. Rxd3? Rxd3 Black would be ahead by four pawns on that exchange (R=5 minus P=1 equals 4 pawns ahead for Black). Therefore, White, with the freedom to make any move he wanted, would almost undoubtedly not want to take the pawn.

*We can see from this example that if a piece or pawn is guarded as many times as it is attacked, it is safe from capture as long as all the guarding and attacking pieces have the same value* (which, as we shall see shortly, is not usually the case!).

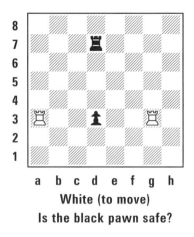

White (to move)

**Is the black pawn safe?**

Now the answer is back to "No." After 1. Raxd3 Rxd3 2. Rxd3 White wins a pawn.

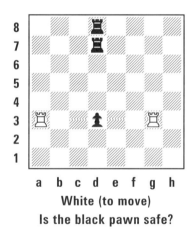

White (to move)

**Is the black pawn safe?**

The answer is "Yes." After 1. Raxd3? Rxd3 2. Rxd3 Rxd3 Black is again up four pawns.

## The Only Time You Are FORCED to Recapture is IF it is the ONLY WAY to Get Out of Check!

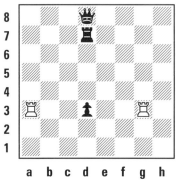

**White (to move)**
**Is the black pawn safe?**

The answer is still "Yes." Substituting a Queen for the black Rook behind the pawn makes no difference, because the Queen can capture last: After 1. Raxd3? Rxd3 2. Rxd3 Qxd3 Black is again up

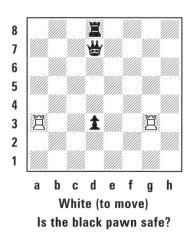

**White (to move)**
**Is the black pawn safe?**

All of a sudden the problem isn't so trivial! With the Queen in front of the black Rook, any recapture must give up the Queen: After 1. Raxd3 Qxd3 2. Rxd3

Rxd3 Black has captured two Rooks (2x5 = 10), but had to give up a pawn and a Queen (9+1 = 10), so the trade is actually approximately even. In this case, the pawn is still considered safe, but a valuable lesson is learned –*it matters what order you can capture (or re-capture) when determining whether a piece is safe.*

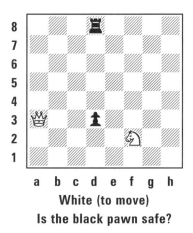

**White (to move)**
**Is the black pawn safe?**

The above example shows that an attacker's order of capture also matters. The pawn is not safe as long as *White properly begins his capturing sequence with his lowest valued piece, the Knight*: 1. Nxd3 wins the pawn. Notice that Black would be foolish to recapture, as 1. Nxd3 Rxd3 2. Qxd3 wins the pawn and "the Exchange" (Rook for Bishop or Knight). White captures 5+1 = 6; Black captures 3, so Black loses 3 instead of the 1 he would have lost if he had not recaptured. Remember, **you are never forced to recapture (unless it is the only way out of check)!** Chess is not like checkers. Beginners almost always make the mistake of making all possible captures on a square once capturing has been started0ed. If White had captured with the Queen first, that would be a huge mistake, as after 1. Qxd3? Rxd3 2. Nxd3, White would lose the equivalent of 3 pawns–a Queen (9) for a Rook and pawn (5+1).

White (to move)
**Is the black pawn on d3 safe?**

All of White's pieces are ready to capture Black's pawn, but the d3 pawn is safe no matter how many times it is attacked by pieces, because the combined value of the defending piece (the pawn at c4), and the attacked piece (the pawn at d3), is less than the value of any piece that can take it. So any capture on d3, such as 1. Nbxd3? cxd3 2. Nxd3 will cost

White the equivalent of 3 pawns (a Knight), while winning only two. Yes, you can capture the pawn on c4, which is not guarded: 1. Nxc4, but that was not the question!

One last example before I let you make up your own:

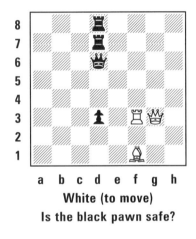

White (to move)
**Is the black pawn safe?**

This very important example shows that you cannot just count up the value of all the pieces that would be capturing on the square (except, of course, the final piece, which captures last and is not taken off the board). White should play 1. Bxd3, and if Black plays 1 ... Qxd3?, then White should play 2. Rxd3 Rxd3 and then White should not recapture, but instead move his Queen to safety, coming out about 2 pawns ahead (getting 9+1 and giving up 3+5). If instead White continued 3. Qxd3? Rxd3, then White would have given up 3+5+9 = 17 and only gotten 1+9+5 = 15, losing the equivalent of two pawns instead! Notice again that White not only does not have to capture 3. Qxd3 on the third move, but he should not. So the pawn is not safe. This example once again shows that *you should only do as much exchanging on a square that is favorable to you; any further exchanges that are not favorable are not forced and thus should be avoided.*

The above example should be sufficient to help the reader set up his own examples. The number of possibile examples are immense (especially when promotion of a pawn is involved!) and the more difficult ones can sometimes even cause an advanced player to pause. Set up some for yourself and practice until you think you (or your student) have mastered "the safety" problem!

## 2.4 Developing Tactical Board Vision Based Upon Rating

In a sense, *any* book on tactics is trying to help a student develop tactical "vision." We can separate tactical knowledge into two admittedly not independent parts:

1) those patterns which contain a tactic, and

2) The knowledge of tactical motifs and how to analyze them to see if there is a satisfactory "combination."

**Advanced Board Vision**

We can also distinguish between beginner exercises such as recognizing tactical motifs such as a pin or fork, and advanced topics such as the necessary preconditions for the *Classical Bishop Sacrifice.* While the latter clearly falls under the topic of "Advanced Board Vision," this section will only deal with developing a beginner's sense of legal moves and beginning tactical motifs.

We need to repeat the level of board vision understanding shown in the previous chapter and develop a corresponding **plan for improvement**:

**1. Under 100 (Level 1):** *Does not yet recognize all the pieces all the time.*

**PLAN**: Players rated under 800 are usually young juniors. They need to play as much as possible. Players under the *100* Level have just learned what the pieces are and cannot even tell what they are. These are usually very young players who just need to be re-assured about all the piece names (relating the names to medieval concepts is usually interesting).

**2. 100-200 (Level 2)**: *Recognizes the pieces, but has trouble remembering how each piece moves.*

**PLAN**: For players just learning how each piece moves it some-times is better not to play with all the pieces at once. For example, just put a Rook on the board and ask the player to name it and show all the places it can move in one move. For youngsters you have to get across the concept that each piece can only make one move at a time, just as each player takes a turn in *Candyland* or check-ers. For Knight moves I often have youngsters stand on a floor with squares and do a "Knight Dance," where each movement is a step two (or one) square in a direc-tion followed by a step one (or two) squares in a direction or-thogonal (at right angles) to the first step. We continue the "dance" until we have tried most of the possibilities several times (like one up and two right; two left and one back; two back and one left, etc.).

**3. 200-400 (Level 3)**: *Has trouble recognizing what the pieces can do, especially with regard to legality, such as mov-ing into check or checking for illegal moves. During a game be-tween two players at this level the board positions tend to be somewhat random. Players at this level often move very fast and "see" almost none of the possi-bilities; i.e., board vision tends to be almost non-existent.*

**PLAN**: For players at this level, playing games with a subset of the pieces is a good start. Play-ers at this level often have con-fusion between checkmate (which involves the concept that you prove you can take the King on the *next* move) and actually taking the King, which is illegal. In other words, they sometimes want to win the game when their oppo-nent moves into check by tak-ing the King. The concept that you not only don't win, but have to "help" your opponent by telling him that his/her move was ille-gal is not trivial. Steve Shutt, the coach at Masterman, suggests that checkmate is best learned by example and suggests a two Rook vs. King endgame. I usually perform that mate with two rulers representing the "force fields" that prevent the King from escaping.

**4. 400-600: (Low Level 4)** *Focuses almost exclusively on his own pieces; usually doesn't consider opponent's possibilities. Therefore puts pieces in take ("en prise") constantly and still makes and allows illegal moves occasionally. Still tends to move very fast.*

**PLAN**: This is the level most people see in youngsters (especially ages 6-8) who say "they can play chess." Because of the way that the brain develops, many youngsters younger than age eight seem to have difficulty understanding that there are two players in every game and both are equally important! They focus exclusively on their moves and rarely look at their opponent's. At this level you make players aware of their opponent's pieces possibilities by telling them to ask themselves:

"Are my pieces safe?," and

"Are there any of my opponent's pieces that are not safe?"

Similar questions would be "If I would move my piece there, can my opponent just take it off for free? " or

"Why did my opponent make that move?"

At this level keeping the pieces safe is the primary tactic, and the player who removes all of his opponent's pieces first either stumbles into a checkmate or draws by stalemating when the opponent is down to just a King. So it is good to introduce the concept of stalemate and tell the player who is overwhelmingly winning that the only way he won't win is by failing to figure out **before he touches a piece** whether his/her planned move allows his/her opponent a move. Getting these players to slow down is also a major challenge. Players at this level should be introduced to the dangers of Scholar's Mate, both defending against it as well as the drawbacks of trying to win with it!

**5. 600-800: (Intermediate Level 4)** *Can chunk some of the board, but doesn't look for alternative moves; still has trouble taking into account the opponent's moves. Still puts pieces in take. Almost all of the game is legal. Tends to move relatively quickly without thinking of consequences of their move or opponent's previous move.*

**PLAN**: This is a common level for bright students 8-10 years old that have played a few hundred games with their family and friends. Being able to understand the concept of counting and almost perfectly execute the concept of safety is necessary for players at this level to progress to more advanced tactics. In other words, in order to progress toward the 800 level, students not only should be able to answer the question, "Is that square adequately defended?," but also to think about piece safety for both players *on* well, even if they cannot execute them consistently. As for openings, they need to know that the three main things you are trying to do are:

1) Develop ALL your pieces,

2) Get some control of the center, and

3) Castle your King into safety.

They should also be able to mate with a Queen and King vs. King and Two Rooks and King vs. King

**It seems that we have busy hands for both colors!**

*every move.* Once they can do so, they are ready to learn the basic tactical motifs from a textbook such as Bain's *Tactics for Students*, which deals with pins, forks, double attacks, removal of the guard, basic back-rank mates, skewers, pawn promotion, etc. Students at the 800 level know at least some of these concepts fairly fairly consistently without stalemating or losing material.

## 6. 800-1000: (Upper Level 4)

*Able to see the board but sometimes misses pieces on the perimeter (such as a far-away Bishop); can make some plans but has no idea what is important in the position. Misses simple mates for both sides and still may put pieces in take occasionally. Still marked by Level 4 understanding; i.e., sees primarily parts of the board and piece moves, but doesn't chunk as much of the position as a Level 5 player.*

**PLAN**: At this level the player should be working through all the basic tactical motifs and should then be able to recognize them in game (and not just problem) conditions. The next step is to start to "combine" motifs, thus being able to pull off basic "combinations." For students with USCF ratings nearing 1000 I like to recommend Reinfeld's *1,001 Winning Chess Sacrifices and Combinations* as they begin to to outgrow Bain's book. Even though 1000 level players will not be able to solve most of Reinfeld's problems, the easiest problems overlap well with the hardest ones in Bain's book. And since tactics are "99% of chess" (Teichmann), progressing through Bain and Reinfeld is a great way to improve their game (from the theory standpoint; from the practice standpoint the best way, is to play as many games as possible against players rated about 200 points above you). One of my students, age 11, improved his rating from about 900 to about 1900 in about 18 months by taking lessons every week, going through the Reinfeld book, and playing incessantly on the *Internet Chess Club*. Players at this level should be able to mate with a King and Rook vs. King well within the 50 Move Rule limit.

**7. 1000-1200: (Hazy area between Level 4 and Level 5):** *For the most part no longer puts pieces in take, but still has difficulty seeing and avoiding simple combinations. Has a tendency to come up with unnecessarily complex solutions to simple problems. Is able to see ahead on the board but still has difficulty understanding what is important in the position.*

**PLAN**: At this level all the players know they have to pay attention to what their opponent is doing every move. Their tactics are rudimentary, but they can hang on and play long games even against fairly good adults. They can solve a higher percentage (but not half) of the problems in Reinfeld's book. High school players who play often are usually at least at this level. Strangely enough, players at this level seem to have trouble following the simple opening guideline, "Move every piece once before you move any piece twice, unless it wins material or prevents losing material." They of-

**Sometimes students really do concentrate**

between two players rated under 1400, there will be at least one point during the game where one of the players will make a tactical mistake large enough to lose the game immediately. Of course, the opponent may not take advantage of the mistake, so it may not decide the game! Therefore, a continued emphasis on tactics, is still a dominant learning theme. Players at this level usually are quite familiar with their opening with White, and also know pretty well at least one defense to 1. d4 and 1. e4. They are also capable of winning many advantageous endgames where they are only ahead one pawn.

ten think that they are "too good" to follow this advice, and 95% of the time they are wrong. Players at this level usually know some opening theory, although often they put too much emphasis on its worth. However, to be fair, a good chess coach should familiarize players at this level with any traps within the player's opening repertoire, so that at least they do not quickly lose to better players in the opening.

### 8. 1200-1400: The beginning of higher level chess.
*Players no longer just win because one gave away more pieces than the other. Level 5 chunking is now becoming apparent in a player's analysis.*

**PLAN**: Players at this level play "real chess" and often can give good games to players up to the expert level. I have a theory that for 99% of games

**Board Vision : Imagination**

## 2.5 Be Imaginative

There is a close correlation between board vision and imagination. But your imagination is not restricted to imagining board positions. Take the following example, which involves understanding how to count how many times a square is attacked:

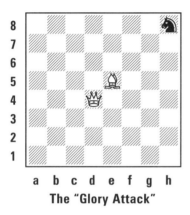

**The "Glory Attack"**

When I am teaching "counting" to the lower rated players, I want them to "see" multiple attacks like the above. However, after asking dozens of students how many times the Knight on h8 is attacked, I was surprised how many answered "one." I began to think about their answer, and decided it wasn't totally wrong. So I discussed this with one of my bright seven-year-old students and we decided to give the attacker behind the initial attacker a special name. He decided to name the indirect attackers after his dog, "Glory." This may sound silly, but now when I teach students about this type of attack and tell the story about Glory, they all remember!...

The above story may seem relatively unimportant, but any gimmick that makes learning fun and interesting is important. It is no coincidence that students quickly learn "Knight on the Rim, You're Future is Dim," but not so easily other similar concepts.

And every student is different. Some learn well by going over games, and a few do not. Some like to go over problems and for others this is drudgery. A good teacher should find out which media the student enjoys and gets the most benefits: books, CD-ROMs, Video Tapes, Audio Tapes, Flash Cards, etc., and try to gear the learning to the student. A visual student will learn better from a book, while an audio learning might benefit more from an audio tape or video tape. And students who are afraid that someone will make fun of them when they lose may have more fun playing against a computer.

# 3: Board Vision and Beginner's Guidelines

The U.S. Chess Federation's *Official Chess Rulebook* has over 300 pages! But that one book on chess *rules* hardly compares with the many books devoted to chess *guidelines*: tips or maxims that help you play better and decide what move is best. This chapter will list quite a few beginner guidelines–most of which are designed to enhance board vision in one way or another–and discuss them in the context of learning chess. Note that these are just guidelines—it is part of an advanced player's ability that he understands the exceptions to these guidelines.

**1) Think and take your time**: This is the granddaddy of all chess maxims. The reason that I call this Guideline Zero when I am teaching is that all the other guidelines are useless if you don't follow this one! One of my young students, who had been taking lessons for months, recently played in his second tournament. He finished all his games before all the other students did, and only managed to win one out of four. After the games I asked him if he had used all the maxims I had taught him. He said no. I replied that all the lessons in the world wouldn't help him play better chess if he didn't take the time to think about what he had learned... Chapter 6 is entirely devoted to the subject of helping students play slower. (By the way, my "Minus One" Guideline is "Have Fun")

**2) Think with your head, not with your hands:** Keep your hands away from the table! You have nothing to win and everything to lose by touching pieces too fast. Remember, serious chess

**Hand hovering-itis**

is played with the touch move rules (if you touch a piece you have to move it; if you let go of a piece you have to leave it there; it you touch an opponent's piece you have to take it)–so there is nothing to be gained by touching a piece before you are *sure* you want to move it.

**3) Before you move, visualize your possible moves and make sure ALL your pieces are safe**; **conversely, look at your opponent's position–if one or more of his/her pieces are not safe, you might strongly consider taking them!** The best way to learn to do that–besides consciously taking your time and looking over the board, is to play hundreds of games, preferably with opponents–computers or humans–strong enough to take

off your pieces when you leave them *en prise* (in take)! Almost all good players learned this way, and after a while you develop the board vision necessary to be careful!

**4) If you see a good move, look for a better one!**–All my students know this one, but only a few actually do it consistently! You are always striving to play the BEST move in any position. So, if you find a better one, don't play that one either–look for an even better one. It is pretty simple logic that you can't prove which is the best move unless you have looked at all of them! As a helpful hint, you should always look at all your potential checks, captures, and threats (and make sure to check to see your opponent's checks, captures, and threats, also!).

**5) You can't play what you don't see**–Until you develop the board vision or the patience to look for all reasonable moves and replies, it is impossible to decide which one is best. Beginners often cannot play the best move because they don't take the time to look all around the board and see the consequences of what they might do.

**6) In the opening, you have 3 main objectives:**

- **Get out ALL your pieces (but not all your pawns):** The sub guideline here is very important thus worth emphasizing: *Try to move every piece (not pawn) once before you move any piece twice.* While this is not always possible (especially when obeying guideline 2–keeping all your pieces safe), it is an important goal. Next to counting (the ability to count captures on a square to calculate safety), this is **the most important opening guideline** I would emphasize to beginners–and some non-beginners. Consider castling a King move so that the castled Rook still may need to be relocated to a better position.
- **Get some control of the center:** Usually by moving a center pawn or two up two spaces and moving your Knights toward the center. Position your Bishops so that they have some control over central squares.
- **Castle your King into safety:** Beginners, and some intermediates, who fail to do this either eventually learn to do so or are consistently beaten by those who do. I am often asked by beginners, "Why is castling so important?" Here are some answers:

Castling is the only move which helps put two pieces at once toward where they should be–so it *gains* a tempo, not loses one.

The King is initially safer toward a corner–the 90 degrees of attack are easier to defend than the 180 degrees in the center.

# King Is Safer In The Corner

The castled Rook can not only get to the center across the rank, but also communicates and coordinates well with the Queen and especially the other Rook.

**7) In the opening, a general order of development might be:**

**"Knights Toward the Center
Then Bishops May Enter
Castle Your King...
Queen up a Little
Rooks to the Middle."**

Don't move more than four pawns, and these should not be Rook pawns, but rather pawns that control the center and/or get your

Bishops in the game. Rooks move to the middle along the first rank–**not** by moving the Rook's pawns up and then moving the Rooks up and over. Also, the Bishop on the side where the King will castle often moves first, then castling, followed by the development of the other Bishop.

The Movement of Rooks

**8) After the opening, when looking for your or your opponent's best move, first try looking at (in order):**

• Checks
• Captures, and
• Attacks ("Threats")–which are usually checks or captures you can do *next* move

This guideline is also the key to finding the most important "candidate" moves in a position (moves that you should consider before deciding on a move). It is also a key to solving most tactical problems. But don't forget to consider YOUR OPPONENT's checks, captures, and threats as well as yours!

**9) As a ROUGH guide, consider Knights and Bishops as worth about 3 Pawns, Rooks 5 Pawns, and Queens 9. Pawns, of course, are worth 1 pawn each:** The key words in this guide-line are "about." The value of pieces changes depending upon the position, and even on the average the above values are only rough. When players get to an advanced level they realize that relying too heavily on these beginner values can be dangerous. For example, a Bishop or Knight is worth more than 3 pawns in many positions, so that a Bishop or Knight plus two pawns is usually worth more than a Rook, and a Bishop plus Knight is usually worth more than a Rook plus a pawn. Unfortunately, some very experienced players never seem to learn this lesson and, as a result, their development is definitely hampered.

Also note that **values** are expressed in "pawns," not "points." I often address students on the value of the pieces and, after I tell them no piece is always worth exactly N (pawns), sometimes they will ask me how many "points" a pawn is worth! So, if you think in terms of pawns and not points, you will not only avoid that pitfall, but also enhance the understanding that you are considering the relative value of material, and not some abstract "points." (If for some reason you want the "advanced" averages, try Q=9.75 pawns; R=5; B=3.25; N=3.25, so "the Exchange" [winning a Rook

> ### *Chart of Values*
> (advanced)
>
> Pawn ................ 1.00
> Knight ............ 3.25
> Bishop ............ 3.25
> Rook ................ 5.00
> Queen ............ 9.75
>
> from Larry Kaufman's
> *Chess Life* Table

for a Bishop or Knight] is worth about 1.75 pawns. These numbers are courtesy of computer chess expert IM Larry Kaufman who published his award-winning article in *Chess Life*.)

**10) Look what your opponent is doing–your pieces are NOT more important than his!:** After your opponent moves, ask yourself, "*Why did he make that move?*"–and don't stop analyzing until you find a reason! Most very weak opponents have *some* reason for making a move–even

if it is not a good reason. An associated question would be "*What can he do to me now that he couldn't do to me before?*" After all, if you properly figure this out each move, then the only new things you need to worry about were generated by your opponent's (or your!) last move. Of course, if you miscalculated what he could do last move, that miscalculation might still exist! Finally, be aware that the new possibilities for your opponent are not just those of the piece he moved, but also any other piece that had a line opened up ("a discovery") by that move. Many errors occur when beginners look at the opponent's moved piece, but not those newly opened lines. Consider the following position:

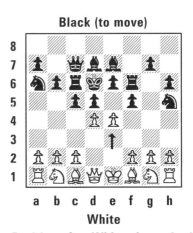

**Black (to move)**

a b c d e f g h
**White**
**Position after White plays e2-e4**

White has just made the pawn move e2-e4. I give this artificial position to beginners and ask them to count and show me all the new moves that White could make *next move* that he couldn't before he played e2-e4 (Black is looking for "threats"—in the form of new White possibilities created by the move e4—to help Black decide what he should do on his turn). The correct answer is that there are 14 new White moves that are now possible: Be2, Bd3, Bc4, Bb5, Bxa6, Qe2, Qf3, Qg4, Qxh5, Ke2, Ne2, exd5, exf5, and e5 mate! Notice that 11 of the 14 moves are the result of open lines created by moving the e-pawn, and not just future moves of the e-pawn itself. It is not a coincidence that the one "straightforward" move that is made possible by moving the pawn to e4, pawn to e5, is designed to be mate! But it is also important that two of the diagonal moves are captures of the black Knights "on the rim." Most beginners will usually not get this apparently simple problem correct without some prompting. This position is a therefore a good illustration of the importance and power of asking yourself *"What can he do to me now that he couldn't do to me before?"*

**11) "Knight on the rim–Your future is dim":** Keep your pieces pointed toward the center–Pieces lose mobility (some of their potential moves) when they are toward the edge—especially knights. In addition, the player who controls the center usually has the advantage; his pieces can get across the board much easier. Knights, being slower than Bishops, Rooks, and Queens, are especially weakened when "out of the action" and are also more likely to be trapped. This guideline is also known as "Knight on the rim –it's future is grim."

**12) When ahead pieces, trade pieces; when behind pieces, trade pawns:** When you have the advantage, trading off pieces leaves you with a bigger percentage lead and reduces enemy possibilities. A lone Bishop or Knight with a few pawns on each side is usually a trivial win, as the piece can coordinate with the King to double attack pawns which the opponent cannot defend, usually resulting in pawn advantages that lead to promotion. On the other hand, when you are down a Bishop or Knight, trading pawns makes the win harder for the player with the advantage, especially if there is the possibility of trading off all the pawns. Loss of all your pawns makes a win impossible, as a lone Bishop or Knight, along with the King, is not sufficient material to checkmate an opposing King.

**13) The more you are winning, the more you should think defense; the more you are losing, the more you should think offense. When winning easily you should make sure you will not lose:** This is a fairly complex guideline and is discussed in more detail in the next Chapter, "Don't Make Lemonade When You Should be Making Ice Tea."

In situations where one side has a large material advantage, it is silly to think that you must spend all your energy trying to get more. In practice, it just makes sense that the side that is winning wants to keep things simple, while the side that is losing wants the position to be complicated. After all, a losing player literally has "nothing to lose" and wants to make the game complicated so that the winning player has more chances to go wrong. If these complications just hasten the losing player's defeat, then at least he tried to get back in the game (you wouldn't take unnecessary chances when behind against a much weaker player, though, because prolonging the game gives him more chances to go wrong...). I have often seen beginners who were ahead a Queen lose because they used their

Queen to go around picking up pawns and, while they did this, their opponent either trapped the Queen or got so far ahead in development that they generated a mating attack. So when you are winning easily, you should follow some of the following practical guidelines to help you preserve your advantage:

**13A) Make sure you don't get mated:** For example, provide your King with "luft," a space to move in case he is checked on the back rank. If your opponent only has one Bishop, the *luft* square is often best on the opposite color of that Bishop.

**13B) Get ALL your pieces out:** This guideline is even more important than it is normally, when it is very important! When you are winning with more material, then bringing all this material to bear on your opponent's position is often more than he can defend. Also, if you bring all your pieces into play, it is much less likely that you will be mated, find yourself short of defense, or find yourself in a bad position because you are behind in development.

**13C) Keep It Simple (KIS):** You don't need complications to win–you're already winning. So avoid crazy sacrifices, or complicated variations. Simple chess almost always wins when you are way ahead.

**13D) Pay attention to what your opponent is doing:** When you are winning, you have a lot to lose, so if you can parry all your opponent's current and future threats, he has a lot less chance of getting back in the game.

**14) If you can keep the game close, then if you outplay your opponent during the crucial tactical portion(s) of the game, you will almost undoubtedly win:** For most beginners, the motto "Whoever makes the next to the last mistake wins" holds true. I have found that telling my students *to pay special attention when things get complicated* is good advice. And they should make sure they have left enough time on the clock so that they are able to pay this attention when that situation arises.

Many guidelines are for particular positions–certain types of endgames, attacks, or maneuvers. Just a few are:

**15) Don't move out your Queen too early.**

**16) Passed Pawns must be pushed.**

**17) Rooks belong on open (or** semi-open) files.

**18) Rooks are powerful on the 7<sup>th</sup> rank.**

**19) In the endgame, the King is a strong piece and belongs in the center. (The King has a fighting "value" of 4+ pawns.)**

**20) Two connected passed pawns on the sixth rank outgun a Rook.**

**21) Bishop and Rook pawn which promotes on the opposite color is a draw.**

**22) A Knight and a Queen work better together than a Bishop and Queen.**

**23) Bishops are better in open positions, Knights are better in blocked positions.**

**24) The Bishop pair is a big advantage (about one-half of a pawn).**

**25) Rooks belong behind passed pawns.**

**26) An attack on the flank is best met by a counterattack in the center.**

**27) See a pawn and pick it**

up, and for the rest of the game you'll have good luck.

28) In middlegame positions with Rooks and/or Queens, move a pawn up to create *"luft"* for your King and prevent back-rank mates.

29) Every pawn push weakens squares.

30) Don't trade off a fianchettoed Bishop in front of your castled King unnecessarily.

31) Bishop of opposite color endgames tend to be very drawish.

# 4: Don't Make Lemonade When You Should be Making Ice Tea

In all chess positions it is important to identify your highest priorities. Unfortunately, books are full of Anatoly Karpov games where exploiting the weak pawn on c5 is the central theme. This emphasis on positional considerations has led far too many weak players to concentrate on little positional nuances when they are up or down a piece! Many guidelines deal with ideas that have very little value when compared to the value of a Knight or Bishop. For example, "Knight on the Rim Your Future is Dim," but if you have to put a Knight on the rim to win a Bishop, it is almost always correct to do so.

In addition, very few books have any detailed advice on how to win when you are up large amounts of material (at least a piece for a pawn) because all good players learn how to do this and it is no longer of interest to them. About the only well known piece of advice given is "When up piece(s) trade piece(s)," which is certainly good advice.

However, many beginners, when up a Queen for a piece (a typical material imbalance!), try to use the Queen to move all around the board picking up stray pawns. Usually what happens is that they lose about 10 tempi and their opponent gets a vicious attack that wins back some of the material.

Even 1200-1400 players are not immune. Often when they are up a piece, they are still worried about doubled or backward pawns, and end up tying up their pieces in a passive position. Or they take the opposite tack and try to start a completely unjustified mating attack.

This leads us to:

## LARGE ADVANTAGE GUIDELINE 1:

**When you are "way up" in material, neutralize your opponents "threats" and the game will usually be over quickly.**

Consider the following position:

**Black**

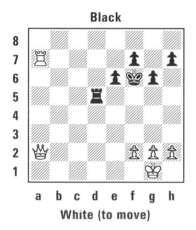

**White (to move)**

White is up a Queen for a pawn and should have no trouble as long as he avoids a back rank mate. With beginners, avoiding a back rank mate may not be enough. Black is hoping to X-Ray (skewer) the King to the Queen or pull off some other miracle. I have seen it happen all too often.

A good player would avoid the back rank mate by 1. h3 or something similar. But following Guideline 1, here is a much safer line of play:

## 1. Qxd5†

White eliminates the only piece that can cause him problems!

## 1. ...        exd5

Now a "normal" continuation would follow the "principle:" "Rooks belong behind passed pawns" and White might try 2. Rd7, which certainly is good. However, allowing 2... Ke6 with tempo leads to a game where Black generates some vague counterplay with his King and his only trump, the passed d-pawn.

So White should say to himself, "What is the only square that can hurt me?" The answer is d1, where Black's passed pawn could promote. But White's King can beat Black to d1. So White should follow the "other" rule: "The King is a strong endgame piece; centralize it and use it!"

## 2. Kf1!        h5
## 3. Ke2        Ke6
## 4. Kd3

**Black (to move)**

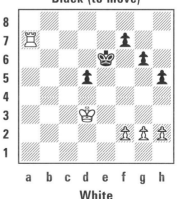

**White**

There you have it! Black can do nothing. Most humans, faced with such a position, tend to get discouraged. When I play this way against my opponents, I often get a quick resignation. Black has nothing to play for, and White, just by advancing his King up the d-file, cannot help but win. Black has absolutely no chance to generate dangerous counterplay.

It is worth repeating what White did. He said to himself, *"I am up a Queen; if I just don't get mated or lose my Queen I can win easily. I don't really need more material. I just have to get rid of the only piece that might hurt me. Let's see, if I take his Rook and then put my King in front of the resulting passed pawn, then I wouldn't want to play Black because there would be nothing left for me to do. Now, let's calculate this again to make sure that it is really that simple... Yes, eliminate the only black piece, neutralize the pawn and win with the Rook. That is what I will do: 1. Qxd5..."*

**LARGE ADVANTAGE GUIDELINE 2:**

**The more you are winning, the more you should think defense first; the more you are losing, the more you should think offense.**

This concept was discussed briefly in Chapter 3, but this advice is so important that we will look at it in more detail.

Telling the player with the better position to think "defense first" seems to contradict World Champion Steinitz' dictum "When you have the advantage, you must attack," but it doesn't. Steinitz was referring to positions where the material was about even but one player had the initiative, for instance due to superior development. In those cases, it is correct to attack, for passive play cannot retain the advantage.

But, when one side has a large material advantage, the opposite is true. If you are up two pieces or a Rook and couple of pawns, and your opponent has no compensation (say in the form of a mating attack), then there are only a few ways you can **lose:**

1) You can **waste a lot of time** moving one or two pieces while your opponent mobilizes his entire force into an attack.

2) You can make **large tactical mistakes** losing material back.

3) You can **fail to safeguard your King,** letting your opponent build up mating possibilities.

4) You can **fail to pay atten-**

tion to what your opponent is doing, thus letting him carry out threats that might not only eliminate your advantage, but give it to him!

So the things you should do to **prevent these losing possibilities** are:

1) **Don't waste time winning a pawn here or there.** Make sure all your pieces are doing something constructive and your overwhelming force will show.

AVOID
WASTING
TIME!

2) **Be extra careful and keep the position simple.** You have more to lose from initiating complications. If you don't give your opponent chances, your extra material will eventually win.

3) **Take time to safeguard your King.** Make *luft* ("light") by moving a pawn up in front of your castled King, preferably creating an escape square that cannot easily be attacked by an opponent's Bishop.

4) **Pay close attention to what your opponent is doing.** Ask yourself:

"What can he do to me now that he couldn't do before?"

"Why did he make that move?" and

"Are all my pieces safe?"

All these factors are essentially defensive. That is okay, since if your opponent runs out of things to do, you will eventually win without having to do anything spectacular due to your large material superiority. Here is an example of the type of tragedy that can occur when you are winning and are only thinking offense:

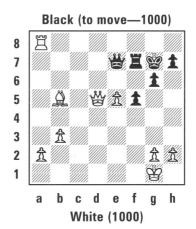

Black (to move—1000)

White (1000)

White, my student, had been attempting to checkmate Black

for quite a few moves. He also had avoided several chances to trade (remember the guideline: trade pieces when ahead pieces). He was thinking "Offense, offense." There are only two ways to lose such a position: put a Rook or Queen in take (or lose it to a simple combination) or allow yourself to get mated. You *can't* plan on not putting your Queen in take, but you *can* try to prevent yourself from being mated, so earlier trades or a timely h3 to give his King *luft* would have been proper defensive maneuvers. Now it was Black's turn, and he played:

| White | Black |
|-------|-------|
| ... | **Qb4** |

Now White should, as always, ask himself, "Why did he make that move? What can he do to me now that he couldn't do to me before?" Instead, I watched White's eyes, which were all on Black's side of the board ("Offense, offense...").

**Be8 ???**

I was afraid of this. Black took very little time to respond and, of course, **did not think defense** by saving his Rook:

| | |
|-------|-------|
| ... | **Qe1#** |

You could see the physical shock go through White. White was not a very young player, but those same eyes which just a few seconds before only could see offense were now welling with tears.

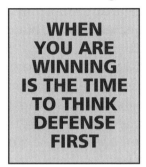

I tried to console him. "It's only a game...If it hurts that means you care and you are more likely to remember this game and be careful so it doesn't happen again. Remember, when you are winning, that is the time to think defense first." My student recovered to win his next two games at this tournament and win a little money. He is now a very fine player and one of my top students.

Now we will consider the same situation, a large material deficit. When you are losing, you should complicate, or attack. When I was a promising teenager, but still inexperienced, Rich Pariseau told me, "I know how to play positions when I am down a piece. I just send all my pieces after his King. If it works, I mate him; if it doesn't, I was going to lose anyway!" Good advice!

When you are losing, you have "less to lose," so trying tricky things is more logical. If you mess up, you probably would have lost anyway. Making the position more complicated raises the standard deviation of what might happen–chessplayers call this "cheapo potential"–and makes it more likely the winning player may go wrong.

**Problems**

I recently heard a quote, "You shouldn't be solving problems when you play chess; you should be giving your opponents problems to solve!" This is only common sense. The more problems you give your opponents to solve, the more likely he will fail to solve one and your position will improve. So if you are losing against a weaker opponent, make moves that would tend to make the game longer (i.e., "give him more problems to solve"), so your opponent will have more opportunities to play worse than you do! You want to be careful not to complicate the situation in a way that is extremely favorable for your weaker opponent should he find a not-so-difficult correct move. That would tend to shorten the game, which is just the opposite of what you want to do. Just don't play too passively, or else even somewhat weaker opponents to make big mistakes.

## SET PROBLEMS FOR YOUR OPPONENT NOT YOURSELF!

**Re-working Your Priorities**

In materially even (or almost even) positions, very strong players adjust their "mental priorities." For example, they know that when they are winning by a pawn, but have other disadvantages, such as being behind in time (development), often there are opportunities to give back the pawn and catch up in development.

But, beginners learn the guidelines given in Chapter 3 and don't know how to prioritize them, not only when the position is almost even, but also when one side is ahead a piece or more.

I sometimes ask beginners if they would weaken their kingside pawns early in the game if they could win a piece. I often use the following position, which occurred during a scholastic tournament, and will be discussed further in Chapter 8:

**Black (1300)**

**White (1180)**
**Position after 7... e4**

If White blunders with 8. Nh4?, instead of playing the better 8. Ne1 I ask, "Is 8... g5 a good move?" It is not a trick question, but many, if not most, answer that 8 ... g5 is not a good move! I tell them that a strong player would not think twice about playing 8… g5 to win the Knight– especially since they are not castled king-side. I then change the position:

**Black (1300)**

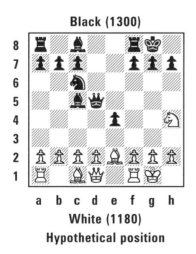

**White (1180)**
**Hypothetical position**

Would …g5 be a good move now? Again beginners are hesitant, but I tell them that winning a piece, in most positions, is far more important than any weaknesses caused around their King. The reasons are several, but the most important is that White does not have any pieces around Black's King to take advantage of the weakened squares and the accompanied King vulnerability. And later, being up a piece, Black should have more "power" left on the board to win the fight to control the squares around his King. So Black is just winning easily after …g5 (not that he has a bad position without it!).

One reason beginners tend to overvalue White's chances in these types of positions is that they are used to playing more "random" chess. And the more random the game, the more big mistakes, and the more critical it is to have the potential for disaster on bad moves. In other words, in this position the weakened King is more likely to be exploited if Black is a very poor defensive player than a strong player. A strong player would know that the King is not very vulnerable in this position and the reasons why (he would easily avoid the kind of moves that might allow White a strong attack). However, weak players might not pay attention at all until it is too late, and then lament the winning of the Knight, even if winning the Knight was not the real problem.

In the above example, we saw that guidelines such as "don't weaken your castled King position by unnecessarily pushing the pawns in front of your King," or "doubled pawns are weak," or "isolated pawns are weak" are all quite secondary to the win of a Knight. Sometimes there are even helpful guidelines, such as "a pawn is worth three tempi (moves)"–so if a Knight is worth about three pawns, then a Knight must be worth about nine tempi! Of course, it doesn't always work this way–in most positions if you gave a strong player nine moves in a row you would be mated even if you took off one of his Knights!

---

### SETTING PRIORITIES SHOULD BE YOUR FIRST PRIORITY

---

All priorities are constantly shifting. Pawns that are "passed" and potential Queens become much more dangerous in the endgame, when there are fewer pieces to stop them. On the other hand, while positional guidelines be-

come less important when one side is ahead material, guidelines about safety become even more important as you have more to lose. In a position where both Kings are exposed to mating attacks, the most important criteria may not be who has the most pieces or pawns, but who has the first move (to start the mating attack!). Just to test some students, I sometimes set up a position and ask "who is better?" without telling them who is to move! I just want them to answer, "whose move is it?" And in the endgame when **King Opposition** is involved, it is usually better if it is NOT your move. Take the following basic example:

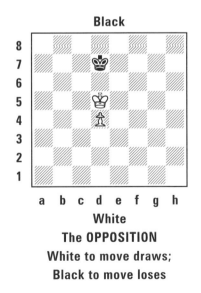

**Black**

**White**

**The OPPOSITION**
**White to move draws;**
**Black to move loses**

For those unfamiliar with this theme, with White to play, a typical continuation might be: **1. Ke5 Ke7 2. Kd5 Kd7 3. Kc5 Kc7** (White is making no progress with his King, so...) **4. d5 Kd7 5. d6 Kd8!** (5... Kc8?? loses to 6. Kc6) **6. Kc6 Kc8 7. d7† Kd8 8. Kd6** drawn by stalemate. But with Black to move, his King must give way and White wins: **1... Ke7 2. Kc6 Kd8 3. Kd6** (the King must lead the way!) **Ke8 4. Kc7 Ke7 5. d5** and the pawn Queens.

Thus, in many sharp middle-game positions (and endgames **not** like the one above!) having the move is often a decisive *advantage*, while in certain endgames like the one above, having the move is a *disadvantage*. No wonder a chessplayer must constantly adjust his priorities! While these adjustments do make chess a more difficult game than most, it is part of the challenge that makes chess interesting and enjoyable. How many books have you seen on Tic-Tac-Toe?

# 5: Know the Rules

One of the most important things you can do when you are learning chess is to know some of the basic rules. By this I don't mean the way that the pieces move, but just some of the most basic other rules, such as the **Touch Move Rule:**

1. **If you touch a piece, you have to move it.**
2. **If you let go of a piece, you have to leave it there.**
3. **If you touch** (or displace with your piece) **an opponent's piece and can take it, you must take it.**

It may sound trivial to say that a player needs to know and enforce these rules, but I have seen the following situation occur several times with both players unaware of the transgression:

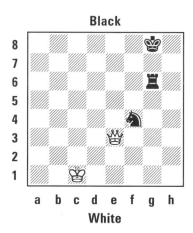

In this simplified version of a typical position Black plays **...Rc6†**, but (properly) does not announce check. The rules do not require you to announce check, although you may. You are never required to help your opponent. I teach my students not to announce check, because as they get better their higher rated opponents will be insulted ("...of course I know it is check. What do you think I am, stupid?..."). In addition, it is part of a beginning player's skill to recognize check, so why not help him learn to look at his/her opponent's moves?

Now, suppose White does not normally look at his opponent's moves, an unfortunately common mistake among beginners. White just sees that Black has not guarded against the threat against the Knight, and therefore plays Qxf4, resulting in the following illegal position:

**Black (to move)**

**White**

At this point Black is sharp

enough to know that White had to get out of check and did not:

"That's illegal."

"Why?" comes the reply from the befuddled White player, still happy over the win of the Knight.

"You are in check!"

"Oh Yeah!" White now puts the Knight back on f4 and the Queen on e3, and instead moves his King to a safe square, say d2. Black in turn is now satisfied that justice has been done and makes another move, for instance retreating his Knight to safety with ...Ng6:

**Black (to move)**

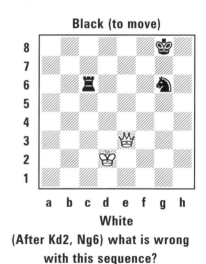

**White**
**(After Kd2, Ng6) what is wrong with this sequence?**

At this point both players are happy, but Black has thrown away an easy win! What did he do wrong?

He forgot that White touched his Queen! After putting the Knight back, Black should have declared "touch move," for then *White has to use his Queen to get out of check*, losing it with Qc5 or Qc3. But Black was satisfied that he had called out the illegal move ruling, forgetting that touch-move also had to be applied.

As mentioned above, this type of error often happens among beginners, and is an excellent example of how a simple enforcement of a known rule can have a large affect on the game.

### Chess is a Game Between Two Players...

Anyone who has seen the movie *Searching for Bobby Fischer* remembers how the parents at the scholastic tournament got locked in the school locker room. This is a slight exaggeration, but the point is clear: chess is a game between two players and the rule is that **No Third Party Can Interfere in a Tournament Chess Game** (with some exceptions for the Tournament Director [TD] or in cases of cheating; see Chapter 10 on Chess Etiquette). Even body language can be informative, and thus illegal. This prohibition on body language not only goes for the obvious, such as frowning just as a youngster is about to touch a piece that would result in a bad move, but also to the less obvious: I try not to stay any longer watching my son's

**Unwanted and illlegal interference**

game whether there is something potentially interesting or not. As a roving tournament director and master, my hovering at a board where an interesting possibility exists could tip off an astute student.

Besides *Touch Move* and *No Third Party Interference,* there are quite a few other rules that a beginner should know, but none is more important than: **If you don't understand what is happening at your chess board (or you and your opponent disagree on a rule), immediately stop your clock and go ask a tournament director**. The TD will not be able to tell you what is a correct move or help you determine a checkmate, but he can tell you the definition of checkmate, stalemate, other types of draws, or pertinent rules.

### TD examples of "problems" from local student play

A few years ago, a young girl, about 10, was playing in one of our tournaments. She was doing fine and was up by more than a Queen, when she suddenly decided that continually checking with the Queen (instead of using her Rook to help) was the right idea. Unfortunately for her, the Queen was not strong enough to do anything but continually

check her opponent's King. Around and around they went. The time limit was to play the entire game in 30 minutes, and when the checking started our heroine had 10 minutes left to her opponent's 15. Her opponent was also unaware of the **3-Fold Repetition of Position** draw rule, or else decided maybe he would try to win on time. In any case, the two players continued to play the same sequence dozens of times without making any claims nor **Stopping the Clock to Ask the Tournament Director,** even though they had been taught not to let strange things happen at their board without seeking advice. I felt bad for the girl, but it was against the U.S. Chess Federation's rules for me to interfere–I would directly affect the result–so I was hoping one of the players would ask me about a possible draw. Neither did. So finally the girl's clock fell and her opponent happily announced he had won on time. Understandably, the girl started to cry at the frustrating loss, when she was easily winning or even drawing, if only she would ask.

The second incident was just as bizarre. One of my seven year old students was playing in a tournament where I was an Assistant TD. I had reminded the parents not to interfere with any games because chess was a game between the two players. I saw that he and his opponent were starting to put the pieces away, so I went over to ask him what happened, expecting him to say, "I lost" or "I won." Instead, I got "I didn't want a draw!" and tears started to well in his eyes. I asked what happened. Apparently his opponent had offered a draw, but had presumptuously stuck out his hand (something I teach my students not to do, as it can lead to situations like this…). My student did not want the draw, but instead of saying "No," had merely shaken hands, as he had been taught by his parents that it was impolite not to shake a proffered hand. He was unaware of the rule that one should should only shake hands after the game is over. His opponent understandably, but mistakenly, thought that the handshake was an agreement to the draw. **(Shaking hands does not end a game.)** To make a long story short, his opponent agreed to continue, but his opponent's father became upset with me for interfering with his son's game– even though I was the TD (for whom some interference is legal) and had only walked over to the game after it was apparently over: putting the pieces away is usually

a dead giveaway! My student, who had been winning, finally won but, due to the misunderstanding over the rules, not everyone was happy.

Although there are hundreds of pages in the rule book, for beginners only a few rules other than those involving the pieces and the clock are required knowledge. For example, when I start teaching someone, I try to ensure that they are aware of **seven types of draws:**

## Seven Types of Draws

1. Agreed
2. 3-Fold Repetition of Position
3. 50-move Rule
4. Both Flags Have Fallen
5. Lack of Mating Material
6. Stalemate
7. "Insufficient Losing Chances"

Most players are not aware of many of these draw rules, but when they are, the most common misunderstandings are:

- Mistakenly thinking that a draw is called a "stalemate." Of course, a stalemate is just a **type** of draw, but *most draws are not stalemates*.
- Mistakenly thinking that a stalemate occurs when the King has no move. I usually point out that in the initial

setup of the game, the King has no moves, so if this were true the game would start as a stalemate! A good way to define it is: **A stalemate is when the player to move is not in check and has no legal move (with any of his/her pieces).**

• Not realizing that the 50-move rule includes 50 consecutive moves by *both players* without a *capture or pawn move* being made by either player.

• Not realizing that a 3-Fold Repetition of Position is **not** the same as 3 consecutive moves (such as moving only one piece back and forth). 3-Fold Repetition of Position means that the same position has occurred (including dynamic posibilities such as castling) with the same player to move 3 times during the game. It could be on moves 72, 85, and 101. Also, if only one player has the same position three times, it is not a draw! **Both** players' position must be the same–else I would try to draw with champion Gary Kasparov on moves 1-5 by moving my Knight back and forth! This rule also means that while "perpetual check" is a legitimate concept, it is not a drawing rule; perpetual check will result **in** a draw when the **same player is to move for the third time in the same position**–IF **the player to move claims the draw before he makes his move.**

## Rules and Misconceptions

Among my students, both young and old, the following is the most common rules that need clarification (except for the drawing misconceptions listed above):

**1. Promotion:** Most beginners seem to think that when a pawn reaches the other side of the board, you can only get back a piece that was captured! Of course, you can get a Queen, Rook, Knight, or Bishop no matter what the situation. Therefore, I commonly ask, "What is the most number of Queens you can have at one time?" When the answer is "9," I know things are okay...

**2. Castling:**

• The King should be moved two squares to either side (many like to move the King *three* squares when castling queenside). *Two is always correct.*

• Similarly, some players reverse the position of the King and Rook when castling (instead of moving the King two squares and putting the Rook right next to the King, but on the other side.

• Some players castle out of

check or through check. Neither is legal.

**Black**

**White**

**Castling through check is illegal—In this position White cannot castle**

- Others think you cannot castle once you have been in check. Castling is still legal if you have not moved your King or the Rook with which you are castling.
3. **En Passant:** Many are unaware of the rule, or miss one or more of the three main ideas. I think it is best described "**If a pawn moves two squares on its first move and an opposing pawn** *could have taken it if it had only moved one square*, **the opposing pawn may capture it just as if it had only moved one square—on the next move only.**" The key ideas (besides the *capture as if moving one*) are:

- The captured pawn must have moved two squares
- Only a *pawn* can take it, and
- Next move only
4. Besides "stalemate" not meaning "draw," there are other **common misconceptions on** chess nomenclature:
- A *Knight* is not called a *Horse*
- A *Rook* is not called a *Castle*
- A *Forfeit* is not *Resignation* (A forfeit is when someone doesn't show up for the game)
- A *Tie* is not a *Draw*: You can tie for 2nd place, or tie a chess match 3-3, but you draw a game. In addition, if three players score 4-1 and you are next at 3-2, you are not 2nd, but 4th, since there are three players with better scores than yours.

---

### TIES
### DRAWS
### STALEMATES

---

- An *attack* (to threaten to capture *next* move) is not the same as a *capture;* we don't *kill* chess pieces. So, the next time you hear someone say, "I killed his horsey," they are probably not a strong chess-player…
- *Tournaments:* Almost all the parents of my students ini-

tially tell me "Johnny is not ready for tournaments." They picture tennis tournaments, where only the best players show up and there is immediate elimination for the losers. Nothing could be further from the truth with regards to chess. Most scholastic tournaments include many beginning players.

Almost all tournaments are held in accordance with the **Swiss System**, whereby everyone plays every round and is paired with someone doing as well as they are. So if a beginner starts the tournament 0-3 (zero wins, three losses), he will usually play someone else who is also 0-3. No one is eliminated.

And every tournament gives out trophies for unrated players (those who have never played before) and many now have trophies for the very low rating classes (such as Under 800, Under 600, and even Under 400) that are common among young players.

When beginners' parents hear the word "tournament," they immediate think *tough competition* and *elimination*. Maybe we should change the name from "tournament" to "festival." If I say, "There is a *Chess Festival* this Saturday; why don't you bring Johnny over to play some games with the other kids?," I am more likely to get a positive response!

## Parent Misconceptions About Tournaments

We mentioned above that parents often think their child is not good enough (or "serious enough") to play in tournaments, when in fact there is no minimum skill level required. This is probably the most common misconception about scholastic chess. The two main things a child *does* need to play in tournaments are:

1) Enough maturity/good behavior to play by themselves, keep relatively quiet, and follow the rules (one does have to know the basics such as checkmate and stalemate), and

2) Enough stamina to last through at least four G/30 (Game in 30 minutes, which last up to 1 hour) rounds, or at least four hours; most tournaments are that long because the USCF requires four rounds to get a rating.

Most children can do this by the time they are seven, but some students of ages five or six play in tournaments regularly.

## Other common misconceptions about scholastic tournaments:

*Misconception #1*: **You have to pre-register to play in a tournament.**

*Fact*: Pre-registration is defined as registering before the day of the tournament. While pre-registration is required in many other activities, most entries are made during a registration period just prior to play **on** the day of the tournament. The exceptions are the really big tournaments, like state, national, and scholastic championships where there are so many entries that it would be impractical to sign everyone up in a short period, so incentives are given to encourage participants to pre-register.

*Misconception #2*: **You have to play all the rounds.** This is a very common misconception.

*Fact*: No one forces you to play all the rounds; sometimes there is a higher priority event that might take you away for a couple of hours. The correct actions if you must leave are:

1) *Notify the tournament director* as soon as you know when you must leave (hopefully, before the tournament begins) and then remind him when you leave.

2) *Notify the tournament director* when you are returning and let him know when you are back. By performing these actions, you ensure that you will not be paired against someone when you are not there. Hardly anyone likes to receive a forfeit win; they came to play. On the other hand, if you leave without notifying the tournament director, he will pair you and someone else who came to play may receive a bye. That is why leaving without notifying the director is against USCF rules, and the organizer is allowed to fine you a small amount before you can enter another of their tournaments.

*Misconception #3*: **Tournaments will provide a board and set for every participant.**

*Fact*: Very few tournaments provide equipment (except for scoresheets)! So at least bring a set, board, and pen/pencil. A standard set is denoted by the "Staunton Design," which is the one used for most sets sold today. The standard size set has a 3.5-3.75 inches high King and is weighted, but such a set is not required. Very small unweighted sets can be hard to handle and easy to knock over. Most players use plastic sets; they are much cheaper than comparably sized wooden sets. If you have a chess clock, bring that, too; if you don't have a clock, you might consider purchasing one. Today the standard chess clock is digital, which can be set with the standard "time delay" feature (where you get an extra five seconds thinking time for each move you make), are more accurate, are easier to read, and probably even more fun! However, digital clocks are more expensive; you can also purchase an older mechanical chess clock. If you don't have a clock and your opponent doesn't either, you can try to borrow one. If that fails, you may start your game without a clock, but the tournament

director reserves the right to give you one during the game so that he can ensure that the next round starts on time. If you purchase a standard rollup (most likely made of vinyl) board, and have a choice of colors, choose a color that is easy on the eyes, such as green. Finally, most participants purchase their own scorebooks, which bind together scoresheets for about 50 games. These are inexpensive, and help to keep game records together for easy retrieval.

*Misconception #4*: **Younger students shouldn't or can't play in clubs or tournaments with adults.**

*Fact*: Many students play regularly with adults, and sometimes beat them! There are quite a few scholastic tournaments that don't allow adults, but most tournaments are "Open" tournaments, in which anyone can play, and many students enter and compete against adults. Chess has no height or strength aspects, so the competition between adults and younger students is often very close. Of course, tournaments that cater to adults usually have slower time limits and expect "appropriate" tournament behavior from all participants (such as no talking when any serious games are in progress), but many younger players play regularly and with few problems.

# 6: Board Vision and Time

Which came first, the chicken or the egg?

Which comes first:
1) Knowing more about evaluating positions, which then requires you to take more time in order to move, or
2) Understanding that taking more time to move is beneficial, and so you take more time and see more?

I would like to think that possibility #2, the realization that taking more time is beneficial, would be the main reason for students to play slower (then I could get students to slow down just by telling them how beneficial it is). However, from my own experience as a beginner and as a full-time chess instructor, I would say that both #1 and #2 are required to slow down most beginners.

**The Tortoise always beats the hare...**

In my first tournament in 1966, I played all my games in about twenty to forty minutes. I was sixteen years old, and the time limit was 50 moves in two hours. I wondered why everyone was taking so long to make their moves. However, at my first three tournaments I only won one game each, so I knew right away that the other participants must have been thinking about something beneficial. As I learned more about chess, I began to slow down. So there was quite a bit of #1 in helping me take my time.

## TORTOISE

*Too Fast – Loses the Thinking Race*
**Takes His Time and Finds
the Right Move**

Many of my younger students like to play their entire game in five to fifteen minutes, no matter how much time they are given. Other players the same age (but admittedly with more experience) play much slower. My fast-playing students almost invariably lose when playing at their normal, quick speed. I call this quick playing *"Flip Coin Chess."* This name implies that the aspect of skill is greatly diminished when so little thought is applied. It is almost as if the two young players are flipping a coin to see who wins. It doesn't matter too much which player has more chess knowledge, because he isn't using it!

Even when my students play fast and lose, they rarely learn their lesson and play the next game slower! This failure to learn is very interesting, and I have tried to understand what it means about human nature, my students, and my teaching methods. For one thing it points out that playing slow is WORK, and WORK is less fun than PLAY. You might think the more powerful emotion is that winning is more fun than losing; yet, so many students would rather "play" and lose than do work and win (but not all students, thank goodness!). It also

**Take your time and win those trophies**

shows that explaining what is happening, even to bright, perceptive students, has very little impact. And age, while a definite factor, is not the only answer; some eight year olds play much slower than some ten year olds. So what does slow down a fast player?

### Playing like a jet doesn't help!

Peer pressure does work. If a fast player plays in a tournament with experienced players who play slowly, he is much more likely to do so, too. Interestingly enough, this even works with open tournaments where young students play adults. The students not only see the benefits of playing slowly, they imitate the "group behavior" and make some attempt to take their time. Conversely, some of my students who have learned to play more slowly will speed up when playing against another student who plays extremely fast, usually with unfortunate results. I try telling my students:

**"The fates gave you your talent and the tournament director gives you time on your clock. You should use both to the maximum extent possible!"**

**"If you don't play slow, your rating won't grow!"**

I also ask my students

**"What if you played a clone of yourself and one of you took 2-3 seconds on each move and the other took 1-2 minutes? How many games out of a hundred would the one playing slowly win?"**

The answer is usually 90-95%, which seems about right (this equates to about 400 USCF rating points, which is about how much strength you would lose playing five-minute versus tournament speed). So if you play fast and another student beats you 9 times out of 10, then you might be just as good as they are if you slow down!

Here are some tips that may help:

**1. Sit on your hands:** Because of the "Touch-Move" rule, there are absolutely no benefits to playing with your hands over the board (except in severe time pressure!). So many chess coaches require their students to literally "Sit on their hands" to prevent them from reaching out and making the first move they see.

**2. Pretend the pieces are HOT and heat up with each move:** Don't touch them until you give them a little time to cool down.

**3. When you see a good move, look for a better one:** This advise is also discussed in the "Guidelines" chapter. Students seem to respond to the idea that you have about 35 moves, on the average, in a chess position, and you are looking for the best one, not the first one your mind sees as enticing.

**4. Write your move down first, and then do a "Sanity Check":** After you think you have found a move, write it down, and then go back and think some more about this move from a fresh perspective: Am I just putting this piece in take? Can my opponent just take one of my pieces? Am I missing something big?

**5. Write down some guideline targets for time on your scoresheet before the game:** For example, if the tournament is Game in 90 minutes, it might be reasonable to use the "Botvin-nik" rule of playing the first fifteen moves in thirty minutes, or even fifteen moves in twenty minutes if you are afraid thirty is too slow. If you play your first fifteen moves much faster that means you are probably playing too fast. The targets on your scoresheet should help remind you to pay attention to the clock. Writing these time guidelines is legal, but writing analysis notes or notes about general strategy (e.g., "Speed Up!")

| opening | | | round no. |
|---|---|---|---|
| | | | date |
| vs. | | | |

| White | Black | White | Black |
|---|---|---|---|
| 1 | | 21 | |
| 2 | | 22 | |
| 3 | | 23 | |
| 4 | | 24 | |
| 5 | | 25 | |
| 6 | | 26 | |
| 7 | | 27 | |
| 8 | | 28 | |
| 9 | | 29 | |
| 10 | | 30 | |
| 11 | | 31 | |
| 12 | | 32 | |
| 13 | | 33 | |
| 14 | | 34 | |
| 15 | | 35 | |

**Sample chess scoresheet**

on your scoresheet is illegal. There is a fine line between what is illegal and what is legal, and the final discretion is up to the Tournament Director.

**6. Write down how much time you** (and your opponent, if possible) **have left after each move:** This can be an invaluable way of helping your chess teacher (and yourself) decide how well you are using your time. For example, if you play a very bad move in 10 *seconds*, you are probably playing too fast. If you make the same bad move, but took 10 *minutes*, then your teacher should examine your thought process to see why you would make such a bad move after "careful" deliberation.

It is always gratifying, to see one of my fast students slow down. The smiles and results are always positive!

There once was a talented young player who played at my high school a few years after I graduated. Even though I was rated much higher than he was, I noticed something interesting. Whenever there was a position where the move looked obvious, but wasn't, he would play slowly. When a position occurred where the move looked difficult, but really wasn't, he would play the correct move rather quickly. This behavior was quite the opposite of the other beginning players! Others would quickly play an obvious-looking move quickly, often with bad results.

This player went on to become a strong FIDE Master and postal player. I never forgot the lesson I learned from watching his games: how long a player takes on a move can tell you almost as much as seeing what move they made…

I often compare the use of chess clocks with basketball referees: it's a different game without them. The element of time in chess is so important that you lose equally whether you get checkmated or use up all your time.

With the recent trend toward faster time limits and "sudden death" time controls–where all your moves have to be played before the flag falls–the emphasis on "time management" has increased. The player that uses his/her clock better has an excellent chance of winning.

In a recent tournament with a time control of Game/45 minutes, one of my best students was playing another good junior player rated just below him. My student, a cautious player, took so much time for the late opening and early middlegame that he reached a complicated position where he had 5 minutes left for all his moves, while his opponent had 35! His opponent was wise enough to keep the position complicated, and soon thereafter my student lost material in time pressure. My student's clock management in that game left a lot to be desired.

> **It is difficult
> to
> speed up
> your play when
> complicated
> tactical problems
> must be solved.**

Decisions in a 2-hour game that take 3-4 minutes need to be decided in 20-30 seconds in a 30 or 45 minute game. It is difficult to speed up complicated tactical analysis, so quicker strategical decisions must be made to ensure that adequate time remains to keep the position "tactically even."

One final reminder: if you have the time, use it wisely!

# 7: Just Because It's Forced...

There is an interesting type of chess mistake that is fairly common among players rated under 1200, although higher rated players sometimes make it, too. This mistake occurs after the opponent makes a move that obviously responds to your threat. You mistakenly think that just because the opponent *had* to make the move, that move's only purpose was to respond to your threat. Therefore, you do not take the time to look for threats caused by the opponent's move. In other words, you think to yourself, *"Okay, he's defended against my threat (or recaptured my piece); now what else can I do to him?"* This poor logic completely skips the necessary thinking step of *"Now, what can he do to me that he couldn't do to me before?"* because the faulty assumption is made that a forced move, or a move that responds to a threat, cannot contain a threat itself.

The following games illustrate this mistake.

| | White | Black | | | |
|---|---|---|---|---|---|
| 1. | e4 | Nc6 | 12. Ne2 | a5 | |
| 2. | d4 | e5 | 13. f4 | exf4 | |
| 3. | d5 | Ne7 | 14. Nxf4 | Nxf4 | |
| 4. | Nc3 | Ng6 | 15. Bxf4 | Ba6 | |
| 5. | Be3 | d6 | 16. b3 | Bxd3 | |
| 6. | Nf3 | Be7 | 17. Qxd3 | Nh5 | |
| 7. | Qd2 | Nf6 | 18. Bd2 | Bg5 | |
| 8. | O-O-O | O-O | 19. Nf3 | Bxd2 | |
| 9. | h3 | a6 | 20. Rxd2 | Nf4 | |
| 10. | Bd3 | b5 | 21. Qe3 | Qf6 | |
| 11. | Nh2 | b4 | | | |

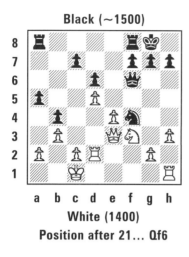

Black (~1500)

White (1400)

Position after 21... Qf6

change.

Here is another example of a game played the same month by one of my top students:

Black has just responded to White's threat to take his Knight on f4 by playing 21... Qf6. White sees that Black has guarded the Knight but doesn't analyze what Black is now threatening because he mistakenly feels the Queen's *only* purpose in moving to f6 was to guard the Knight. Of course, Black just happens to also now be threatening 22... Qa1#!

White proceeds to set up a pin on the Knight, continuing the offensive, but completely missing any defensive idea:

**22. Rf2??**

White was just completely lucky that his "offensive" move contained the defensive power of stopping the mate.

| | White (1900) | Black (1700) |
|---|---|---|
| 1. | c4 | c5 |
| 2. | g3 | Nc6 |
| 3. | Bg2 | Nf6 |
| 4. | Nc3 | e6 |
| 5. | e4 | Be7 |
| 6. | Nge2 | Rb8 |
| 7. | d4 | cxd4 |
| 8. | Nxd4 | d6 |
| 9. | e5? | Nxe5 |
| 10. | b3 | b6? |
| 11. | f4 | Ng6 |
| 12. | Nc6 | Qc7 |
| 13. | Nxb8 | Bb7 |
| 14. | Nb5 | Qxb8 |
| 15. | Bxb7 | Qxb7 |

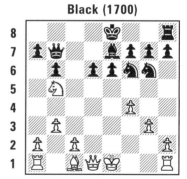

Black (1700)

White (1900)

Position after 15... Qxb7

| 23. | ... | Qa1† |
| 24. | Kd2 | Qxh1 |
| 25. | Qxf4 | |

...and Black has won the Ex-

Black has just been forced to take on b7, so White, a very good

player, forgets to look at his opponent's "long-range" threat of 16... Qxh1†. Therefore, after 16. Nxd6†?? Bxd6 White was lost as he couldn't both recapture the Bishop and guard his Rook.

This example illustrates another point. Moves that threaten across the board, especially diagonal moves, are easy to miss. You have an excuse in a "speed" game, but in slower chess sometimes you just have to "look around."

The following diagram is another example of this chapter's theme:

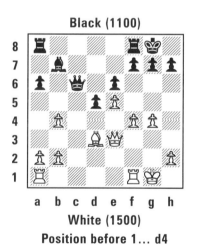

**Black (1100)**

**White (1500)**
**Position before 1... d4**

Black so far has played a nice game against his much higher-rated opponent. He now correctly opens the long diagonal with **1... d4,** threatening mate on g2. White was expecting this move and played **2. Qh3,** defending against the mate, but also... Black thought

for a while and played **2...Qh1†??** One principle (?) is "Always check, it might be mate!," but it is not really a very good guideline, and this is an example! After 2... Qh1†??, White is forced to play **3. Kf2,** threatening the Queen on h1 *and* the mate on h7. Black, who had not seen the mate on h7 because he thought the move 2. Qh3 was simply guarding g2, now retreated his Queen from h1 and was surprised when he was mated with **4. Qxh7#.**

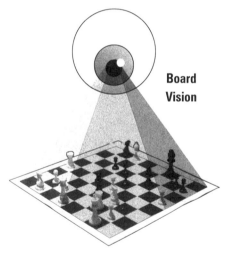

**Board Vision**

Board vision problems are not limited to the young. In the next example my student is retired, but he falls prey to the same problem my younger students exhibited above.

Black (1100)

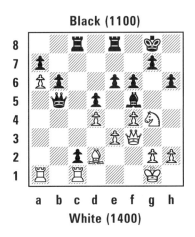

White (1400)

of my students:

Black (1100)

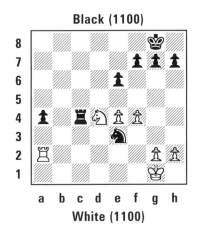

White (1100)

In this position, Black has lost a piece for two pawns against a higher rated opponent, but the game is not over. Having just driven the Knight out of e5 with ...f6, he feels compelled to attack it again:

| White | Black |
|-------|-------|
| ... | h5?! |
| Nf2 | e5? |

Black reasoned, "I know why the Knight went to f2; it was to avoid capture by the pawn with which I just attacked him." As the reader should know by now, a move that was forced also may contain a threat. White of course played...

**Qxh5**

...and went on to win.

Here is yet another example of this common mistake from a tournament game between two

White is lost, as Black is skewering his Knight and e-pawn. However, at this level anything might happen, so he tries to counterattack:

| White | Black |
|-------|-------|
| Re2 | Ng4 |

Black's Knight is attacked, so he retreated it to the most reasonable square. Naturally, but incorrectly, White is not worried about the offensive aspect of such an obvious retreat...

| Nb5?? | Rc1† |
|--------|------|
| resigns | |

It is mate on the back rank on the next move, as the "retreat" ...Ng4 also covered the King's only escape square, f2.

In the above examples, the defender was simply making a forced move and was "lucky" that his opponent made the mistake of not looking for other threats that the forced move created as a by-product. However, the astute player can also consciously use the tendency of his opponent to overlook the offensive threat of defensive looking moves. Here is a cute example from one of my games:

| White (1700) | Black Heisman |
|---|---|
| 1. e4 | c5 |
| 2. Nf3 | e6 |
| 3. Nc3 | Nc6 |
| 4. b3 | d5 |
| 5. exd5 | exd5 |
| 6. Bb5 | Nf6 |
| 7. O-O | Be7 |
| 8. Ne5 | Qc7 |
| 9. Re1 | Be6 |
| 10. Bb2 | O-O |
| 11. Bxc6 | bxc6 |
| 12. Qf3 | Rfe8 |
| 13. Ne2 | d4 |
| 14. Nf4 | Bd5 |
| 15. Nxd5 | cxd5 |
| 16. c3 | dxc3 |
| 17. Qxc3 | d4 |
| 18. Qh3 | Bf8 |
| 19. Nf3 | Qf4 |
| 20. Qh4 | |

My opponent is much lower rated and is playing for a draw. So far, I have done nothing to demonstrate why I have a higher rating, but the next few moves I show signs of thinking.

| 20. ... | Qf5 |
|---|---|
| 21. Ba3 | h6 |

When playing ...h6, which defended against some later Ng5 threats, I began to notice that my opponent's Queen was awkwardly placed. Unfortunately, there was the problem of completely ensnaring the Queen by covering all the escape squares. I then realized that if my opponent continued to attack the "backward" c-pawn, I might be able to make the rare "offensive" defensive move.

**22. Rec1**

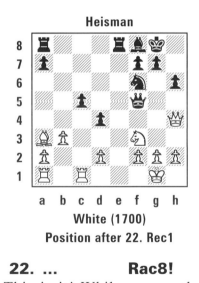

Heisman

White (1700)
Position after 22. Rec1

| 22. ... | Rac8! |
|---|---|

This is it! While apparently overprotecting my c-pawn, I create a deadly threat. I actually made this move rather quickly so that my opponent would think I was just responding to his pressure on the c-pawn.

**23. Rc4?**

...which my opponent, somewhat justifiably, misses.

**23. ...          g5!**

**24. Qg3          Ne4**

The door is shutting. The apparently innocuous 22...Rac8 covered the crucial c7 escape square. So White is forced into...

**25. Qh3          g4**

**26. Nh4          Qxf2†**

**Resigns**

The conclusion from all of the above examples (and many more not shown–this is a common mistake!) is the same: Whether you are an experienced player or not, you always must be aware that *your opponent's move often does more than just its seemingly main purpose*–so be on your guard!

# 8: Assume the Best

Take a look at the following position:

**Black (1300)**

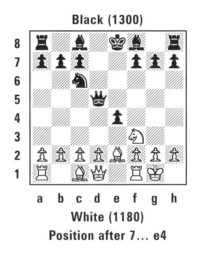

**White (1180)**
**Position after 7... e4**

This position was reached after the moves **1. e4 e5 2. Nf3 Nf6 3. Nc3 Nc6 4. Be2(?) d5 5. exd5 Nxd5 6. Nxd5? Qxd5 7. 0-0? e4.**

Up to this point White has made several small mistakes: he met the Petroff's Defense with the passive but acceptable 3. Nc3; he chose the least aggressive post for his Bishop with 4. Be2(?); in trying to avoid doubled pawns he brought Black's Queen powerfully to the center with 6. Nxd5?; finally, he erred by allowing Black's e-pawn to advance by playing 7. 0-0?

In this position an experienced player would reason thusly: "My Knight is attacked and I have no worthwhile counterattack, as 8. c4? would create a weakness for nothing, and my problem with my Knight would still not be resolved. 8. Nh4 seems to lose a piece to 8...g5, when the weakening of Black's kingside is trivial compared to my loss of a piece. 8. Re1 temporarily sets a trap that works if he takes my Knight, but he doesn't have to take it next move; if he just plays safe, then I will lose my Knight. Therefore, I must play 8. Ne1.

White, who at that time was a promising but raw tactical player who primarily had played weaker opponents, went through the first part of this analysis, but stumbled when he considered 8. Re1. Accustomed to opponents who routinely fell into his traps, White apparently thought, "The retreat 8. Ne1 is to be avoided, if possible. I will set a trap by playing 8. Re1; If he plays 8... exf3??? then 9. Bxf3† wins the Queen! Then I won't have to retreat my Knight."

The problem with this logic is that it assumes the opponent won't make the best move! This works well if the opponent is very weak or the best move is very difficult to find, two conditions that exist a lot less often than many players would think! In the above game, Black was actually the better player (which White knew, from their ratings). Black thought for only about 10 seconds to decide on his reply; after all, even if he hadn't seen the trap beforehand, it is not difficult to say to oneself, "He is leaving a Knight *en prise!* What will happen if I just take it? I lose to a check! So I will just stop the check and his Knight will have no place to go!" Black played 8... Be7, won the Knight, and won the game easily.

White, partly through the bad experience of this game, quickly came to realize that he would play quite a bit better if he assumed his opponent *would* find the best reply. As a teenager, he was better equipped to handle the lesson learned from the above example.

Very young children (7 and under), however, often have trouble considering their opponents' moves. The young child makes easily parried "threats," reasoning, "I will go here to threaten his Queen and, after my

**Kids having fun**

opponent makes a move, I will take it off!" The youngster assumes that their opponent, like themselves, will ignore *their* opponent's (the youngster's) moves, and that any threat is reasonable as it is likely to get ignored by their opponent and thus executed on the following move. This faulty logic is reinforced by young opponents who, using the same faulty logic, makes it come true! Unfortunately, when faced with slightly older or more experienced opponents, the young player often just loses material as his/her "threat" is met by. For example, their opponent might be able to just capture the piece which was threatening the Queen.

In the above example, it was not enough that an opponent's piece is unsafe on the *next* move if the opponent can capture the attacking piece *this* move! Inexperienced players do not have the board vision, experience, or (often) patience to check to see if all their pieces are safe. Their sophistication of play and playing strength would increase immensely if they just checked their opponent's last move and said:

"What can he do to me now that he couldn't do to me before?," or

"Why did he make that move?" —and didn't start thinking about their reply until they at least came to some reasonable answer (sometimes the answer is, "My opponent has blundered").

Assuming that your opponent will make his best moves causes you to play slowly. For each move that you are considering (and to find the best move, you must seriously consider any reasonable move), you cannot judge how good the resultant position is unless you figure out what your opponent is likely to do. This task can range from trivially easy ("...there is only one way he can get out of check...") to enormously difficult, depending upon the position and the opponent. But one thing is clear: until a beginner learns to do this on every move, he will be constantly defeated by opponents that do.

To show how important it is to assume best moves in order to correctly evaluate a position, consider the following silly counterexample. Suppose Karpov is playing Kasparov, and Kasparov is up a pawn with a good position, and it is his move. Suppose someone asks me, "Who do you think is winning?" Would it make any sense to answer, "Kasparov is up a pawn with a good position, but Karpov is winning because I think Kasparov is going to put his Queen *en prise*!"?! No? But that kind of illogic is what happens when you do **not** assume that best play will happen when evaluating a position.

From the above discussion (and others in this book), we can conclude that to play "non-beginner" chess, a player has to *at least* do the following:

1) **Take the time** to figure out why the opponent made his move, and which threats created by that move (or left over from the previous moves!) have to be parried.

2) **Try to visualize** possible moves before touching a piece.

3) **Make sure all your pieces are safe** before you move, and that if opponent's pieces are not safe, that you consider their capture.

4) If, **you see a good move,** look for a better one.

5) **Assume the opponent will make the best reply,** and try to figure out for each of your possible moves what the opponent's reply would likely be (and whether the opponent's reply might create a threat that cannot be parried).

The first four above are absolutely mandatory to move above the beginner's level. The fifth is a little more sophisticated, but still essential for any serious progress.

## The Three Levels of Chess Thought

The above touches upon some problems that beginners have in their thought process. The following examines this phenomenom in more detail.

Recently a student, rated 1100, played in a tournament in which his playing strength was 1900 (!) for six rounds. He beat four players higher rated than anyone he had ever beaten before.

As a chess full-time instructor, I was very intrigued as to what had caused this sudden great jump in playing strength. Could it be attributed to random chance or just "having a good tournament?" I have a two-part explanation:

• The first part requires a definition of three levels of chess thinking. The ascendancy through these levels reflect the maturing of a chess player:

**"FLIP-COIN" Chess:** A move is played quickly and without serious thought. The winner of a game where both players are playing Flip-coin chess is almost random, and thus I named it after a coin flip. If one

player plays flip-coin chess and the other actually takes time to think, the thoughtful player almost always wins. Flip-coin players don't use the important guideline "If you see a good move, look for a better one." Almost all young beginners start by playing flip-coin chess.

**"HOPE" Chess:** This is NOT when you make a move and hope your opponent doesn't see your threat. Instead, Hope chess is when you make a move and don't look at what your *opponent* might threaten on his next move, and whether you can meet that threat on your next move. Instead, you just wait until next move and see what he does, and then hope you can meet any threats. In my first three tournaments I played Hope chess and never won more than one game in any of the three. The speed at which you can play Hope chess also explains why I played too quickly.

**"REAL" Chess:** You select candidate moves and, for each, you anticipate and evaluate all your opponent's main candidate moves (especially all checks, captures, and threats). If you see a threat you cannot meet, you cannot play that candidate move; instead, you must choose a can-

didate move that allows you to meet all threats *next* move. One goal of *Real chess* is to anticipate each of your opponent's moves–if you have a good opponent and he makes a move you hadn't even considered, that is not a good sign! This anticipation takes some time and real effort, so all good chess players take their time!

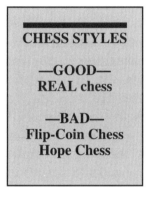

The best way to introduce the second part of my explanation is to make an analogy. Suppose you build a house where the temperature is –20°F outside. You settle on a one-room home with four walls, a roof, a floor, and a heater. You decide to save a little time and material by finishing the four walls, the floor, and half the roof, but the other half you leave open. Even though you have completed over 90% of the structure, the temperature inside your house will still be about –20°F with half your roof open. If you want your inside heater to be effective, you have to enclose all of your house.

This "cold house" analogy is similar to what happens when you play *Real chess* for 90% of your moves, but not for the other 10%. You think you are a good player, but weaker players beat you when you let down your guard during that 10%. In order to be a good player, you have to at least try to play correctly *(Real chess)* on every move, not just most of them.

As an example, my son Delen was playing in the World Open in 1998. He won his first four games in the Under 1400 Section and was doing well until around the seventh round. He was playing a 1300 player and had outplayed him up and down the board for the first 50 moves. He had an easily won endgame, he was ahead the Exchange and a couple of pawns. At that point his opponent checked him and, even though he was in no time trouble, he immediately moved his King to a square where his opponent could then fork the King and his Rook, thus losing the Rook and the game. Dad almost had a heart attack, "How can you play like an 1800 player for 50 moves and then like a 400 player for one, throwing the whole game away?!"

My son replied, "I can't work hard on every move; it's too much effort!" Aaagh! This situation is similar to working hard on a beautiful painting for three weeks and then, in a bad mood, suddenly throwing paint all over it! Once the damage is done...

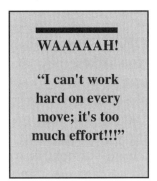

WAAAAAH!

"I can't work hard on every move; it's too much effort!!!"

Now you have all the information as to why the 1100 player had a 1900 tournament:

- He knew about "Real chess" thinking, but until that tournament was still playing some Hope chess.
- He finally realized that, in order to beat much higher rated players, he needed to play real chess on every move, and not just on most of the moves. So, like the cold weather home, when you don't play Real chess on every move, there is a dramatic difference in your rating.

My explanation is more than

just a theory. I did talk to my student and ask him if the above made sense, or was I way off the mark. He replied that it was a pretty good explanation of what had happened. In the next tournament, he continued to play very well, so I am pretty sure he is now playing *Real chess.*

So that is the secret of **Real chess,** you must:

1) make sure that your think deep enough to ensure that you can make it to the next move without facing threats you cannot meet, and

2) do this every move, not just most of them.

Can this "secret" take you from 1800 to 2400? Of course not. As any high rated player knows, there is a lot more to chess than just trying hard and taking your time. But *not* playing *Real chess* can keep your rating a lot closer to 1000 than to 2000.

# 9: Don't Believe Him!

When playing a high rated player, there is sometimes an amount of "bluffing" that may occur. Your opponent may offer a sacrifice that may or may not be sound and you have to use your judgement as to whether you should take the material.

Closer to the beginner level, the problem is somewhat reversed. Opponents are always making mistakes, and a player needs to recognize these mistakes. Often I see games between two lower rated players where one player offers material based on some miscalculation and his opponent declines to take it, figuring that if someone is offering something for free, it can't be good! Of course, in many cases, it is just a blunder and you should take it, saying (to yourself) "Thanks!"

**Black (1350)**

**White (1400)—Black (1350)**
**Position after 11... b5?**

In the above position Black has just responded to White's threat to capture on e4 with 11...b5?. Now it is true that ...b5 still allows a strong capture on e4: 12. Bxe4 dxe4 13. Qxe4 Bb7 as in the game, when White should play 14. cxb5 axb5 (or 14...Na5 15. Qg4) 15. Qg4 and White is better. However, there is no reason to believe that Black's move is a good counterattack. The even more simple 12. cxb5 axb5 13. Bxb5 attacks Black's Knight and leaves White with the Bishop pair and a solid passed a-pawn.

After the game I asked White why he didn't simply take the b-pawn. He replied that he believed Black's threat and thought that the black Rook would be able to menace his Queenside (a lá the Benko Gambit) from b8. I call such groundless fears "Phantom Threats."

It seems the ability to differentiate between real and phantom threats is a real problem for players in the range 800-1600.

### Phantom Threats

Phantom threats occur because of laziness or haziness. An inexperienced player does not try to logically calculate all the possibilities. Instead, he takes "shortcuts" in thinking, like "my opponent's Queen may try to get me. So maybe I will move up that pawn so the Queen cannot go there." In doing so, the beginner doesn't actually calculate whether or not the opponent's move is reasonable, or even a real threat. He just decides to come up with a rationale for a move, and convinces himself that the move is the best one without any real analysis.

When I ask a low rated player to think out loud, they almost always include quite a bit of "hazy" thinking. They don't try to systematically look at their opponent's checks, captures, or threats from the previous move. They don't always consider all their own checks, captures, or threats, either. Because of this, they often "believe" their opponent's last move and respond to it whether or not it made any sense or carried any real threat.

**Phantom threats**

More experienced opponents, seldom "believe" their opponent's move, but instead check the variations themselves to see if maybe their opponent should just be allowed to carry out their "threat," since the variation may be good for them, and not for their opponent!

Here is a typical example from

one of my student's recent games:

**Black (1050)**

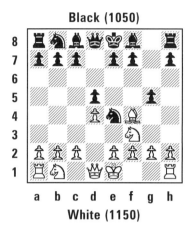

**White (1150)**

My student is White, and Black has just played 4...g5?. I am so used to looking at these types of strange moves with my beginning students that I expected White to play almost anything except the obvious and good 5. Nxg5. I have seen so many 500-700 level players respond to a move like 4... g5 by retreating the Bishop that I have almost come to expect the non-logical retreat. There are two reasons these lower rated players give to justify the Bishop retreat. It is either "My Bishop is attacked by a pawn that is guarded; therefore I must retreat or *lose* the Bishop," or "If I take the pawn, then he will *trade off* my Bishop (Knight), and I don't want to trade." They don't see the capture as just a series of exchanges that win a pawn. Moreover, lower rated players almost always take with the Bishop, because that is the attacked piece. Giving up the Bishop Pair (worth about one-half of a pawn!) for no reason is not correct. However, in this case White, rated 1150 and not 650, did just what he should have done and played 5. Nxg5. I was somewhat surprised!

For players with *very* low ratings, it is usual not to even look at or calculate your opponent's threats. For example, I have seen the following type of position a thousand times (or so it seems!) in beginner's games:

**Black**

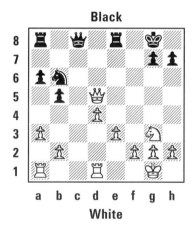

**White**

White has just played his Queen to d5 and announces "check"! Black hears that dreaded call and "sees" that indeed, the line between the Queen and his King indicates his King is in danger (a "check"), so immediately out comes his/her hand to touch the King, and then, after grabbing it, comes the pause as Black decides onto which square the King should move. In other words, they believe that White has made a (safe) fiercesome move, and immediately reacts defensively.

Afterward, I re-setup the position and ask the black player, "What are the three ways to get out of check?"

Black can often dutifully reply, "Move the King to a safe square, put something in the way, or take off the piece that is checking you."

I then ask "Of those ways, which do you think might often be the best?"

To this question, they *will* think and answer, "I guess taking off the piece."

"Well, in this position what do you think is the best way to get out of check?"

Faced with the reality of their previous replies, eyes will now wander over the board as if seeing the position for the first time, and those same eyes will undoubtedly discover that the checking Queen could have been removed for free by the Knight on b6. So out comes the sheepish reply, "I guess Nxd5."

"Then why didn't you take the Queen instead of moving your King?" I know the answer, but I want the youngster to think about what he did, so as to better remember and not repeat the mistake.

A quiet voice replies with a smile, "I guess I didn't see it."

"You have to look. After all, *you can't play what you don't see.*"

# 10: Chess Etiquette

According to legend, someone once asked Bobby Fischer, who is not only famous for being a great chess player but also famous for being "difficult," if he liked to bother his opponents.

"Yes!" Fischer immediately answered.

Sensing a juicy answer, the questioner quickly followed up, "And what do you do?!"

"Oh, I make good moves!"

Not many of us can make good moves like Bobby Fischer, but everyone should know about chess etiquette. Sometimes it is hard to find this information, but sooner or later most tournament players figure it out–sometimes the hard way.

Some chess etiquette is so important that it is written into the official rules. If that is the case, then we will mark that advice with an extra (R) below to denote "Rule".

### All the Time vs. Formal Play

We can separate etiquette into two types: etiquette that applies all the time, whether in a friendly game or serious one, and etiquette that is more particular to tournament play. In a tournament, if you have any question about the rules, including enforcing etiquette, you may stop the clock (if you are using one and it is your turn), and ask the Tournament Director (TD). The US Chess Federation (USCF) certifies TD's, who are not representatives of the USCF, but must enforce/follow the USCF rules or they may lose their USCF license to run rated tournaments.

## ALL THE TIME

The following etiquette rules apply all the time:

### Talking is a no-no

Don't bother your opponent in any way. This rule (R) takes many forms, from asking questions (even when it is your move, your opponent also has the right to think on your time!), making noises, talking loudly or unnecessarily with others, moving the table or pieces, making distracting motions, displacing the clock, obscuring the board, anything your opponent legitimately finds distracting (and most US tournaments have "No Smoking" in the playing conditions). The list could go on for an entire book! But most importantly, I should repeat, Chess is a Quiet Game!

Chess should be played without talking (the exceptions are draw offers, indicating the stopping of a clock, on your own time (or move), to get the TD, adjusting pieces on your move, indicating a rules' violation such as touch move, and emergencies. (Calling "check" is optional–see the paragraph below about Calling Check). Of course, if he finds your quiet breathing distracting he should purchase a good noise protection device and not pester the TD to stop you from breathing...

### Greet Opponent

Always greet your opponent at the start of a game. A handshake and a friendly "Hi, my name is ____" is the very minimum. Most players, at the start of a tournament game with an unfamiliar opponent, check the player's name (and rating!) to see if they are playing the correct player, and make a little small talk such as asking how the opponent is doing, where are they from, and even wishing them "Good luck" (even if they don't really mean it!) etc. Usually a handshake (or sometimes a second one if it has been a while since you both first sat down) preceeds the starting of the clock. Black is expected to start the clock so that White can move, but White may move immediately and start the clock (R).

### Resigning

The president of my first chess club gave me the following advice, which I will paraphrase:

"Dan, you are a beginner. Our club has many fine players who will be willing to play you. When you play them you have two choices if you are losing to a much better player. If you reach a position where YOU could beat THEM easily, the proper thing is to resign and thereby not insult them as to their ability to checkmate you nor waste their time. However, if you are curious as to how they can best checkmate you, you may play the game out to checkmate, but it is considered bad manners to make them play all that extra time and then resign right before checkmate, so let them mate you."

I should hasten to add that if you are playing a player considerably worse than you are, you should be hesitant about resigning too soon. If you are playing an absolute beginner, he may have no idea at all how to checkmate you from a superior position and many will stalemate you or draw through the fifty-move rule, so I wouldn't resign against beginners at all.

By the way, there are several ways of resigning:

You can say "I resign," or

"I give up,"

You can lay down your King, or

You might just reach out to silently stop your clock and offer a handshake.

A word of warning, however. Handshakes end the game. If someone offers you a draw (see **offering a draw** below), you may say "I accept" or offer your hand as a signal of acceptance. To decline, simply say "I decline," "No," make a move, or say "let me think about it," after which you may do any of the others. (R)

A young student of mine did not know that shaking hands ends the game, and since he was brought up to always shake an offered hand, he did so! The other player was nice enough to continue the game, but the lesson is clear: "Don't shake hands unless you agree the game is over!"

### The Way of Moving Pieces

Some players like to intimidate their opponents by banging down their pieces to emphasize a good move. Others like to screw the pieces into the board. Any similar behavior is viewed unfavorably by the majority of chess players. If you have an opponent who consistently does these things to an annoying degree, you may ask the TD to request that your opponent stop doing so.

### Answering A Request to Play a Game

Recently I was at my local chess club there were only three strong players present, two others and myself. The other two were playing a short game. I asked if I could play the winner. The players vaguely nodded their assent and I awaited the finish by walking around the club. When I came back, the game was over, but the players were analyzing the position. I helped them analyze for a while, but they wanted to continue to analyze, so I again strolled around because I didn't want to interfere. A few minutes later I came back and they had started another game! I considered this quite rude, as it was obvious that the players had waited for me to walk away so they could continue to play each other. If they *did not* want me to play the winner, it would have been correct etiquette for them to simply answer my request, "No thanks, we just want to play each other this evening." I would not have been upset if they had done this. If they *did* want me to play, I was only within 20 feet of their game, so it would have taken very little effort to locate me. But *not* clearly turning down my request combined with *not* letting me play (I could have played a weaker player instead of waiting) was clearly a breach of etiquette.

There is also the question of game conditions. In a tournament these are clearer, but informally there is the question of using a clock (some beginners are vehemently opposed) and, if so, how long the game should be. Normally these things are easily

worked out. However, if you are playing without a clock and your opponent is taking too long, welcome to the club! Maybe next time you will want to play with a clock, too. As to the other conditions, normally chess is played with a Staunton design set (R), and if there is more than one game the players will alternate colors. If you play White first and win quickly (so that there is still plenty of time for more games), it is especially considerate to offer to let the other player have White, too, and not just seek a stronger opponent.

## FORMAL CLOCK PLAY
### When to Stop the Clock

There are only two correct times (R) to stop the clock:

1) When the game is over, and

2) When one of the players is on the move and he wishes to ask the TD a question about the rules.

If you have to go to the bathroom, just make your move, push the clock as normal, and go to the bathroom. It is also considered incorrect (R) to touch the clock during play. For example, you should not rest your non-moving hand on the clock, nor should you pull the clock in front of you to read the time remaining. Occasionally, players are allowed to angle the clock momentarily toward them to better read the time remaining, but they should not do so if their opponent is about to hit the clock, and they must return the clock to a position that is equally accessible to both players.

By the way, people who have never played with a clock before often forget to hit the clock after their turn. It is polite to remind them a few times early in the game, at least often enough so that they should get the idea. However, there is no requirement for you to help your opponent, and if he forgets to hit the clock during time pressure, you do not have to let them know. Just think normally; if your time is short and you are not moving quickly, most opponents will look at the clock and realize they forgot to hit it. If they get upset, they should be upset with themselves for not hitting the clock, and not you for not telling them. It is their responsibility to hit the clock, not yours to tell them if they didn't. In one of the crucial Kasparov— Karpov World Championship matches, Kasparov was in time trouble and did not hit the clock. Karpov correctly did not tell him and, when a minute later Kasparov realized his error, he was upset. However, it seemed to me that Kasparov was upset with himself for making such an elementary error, and not at his long-time foe for not telling him.

## THE DRAW
### Offering and Accepting a Draw

There is only one acceptable time to offer a draw (R): after you move, but before you push the button on the clock. Since there is a responsibility to move, if your opponent offers a draw while he is thinking, you should politely ask him "please make your move and I will consider it." Because he made an illegal offer, he is not allowed to withdraw his offer, even if he finds a move that convinces him that he is winning, nor may he threaten to withdraw his offer if you don't take it immediately.

Once, not soon after I started playing tournaments, I offered a draw during my move to a master whom I had beaten previously. The above rule was not in effect in those days, so the master, who was looking for revenge, immediately said no. I then found a winning continuation and played the winning move. The master thought for a while, smiled, and humorously asked, "You still don't want that draw, do you?" I smiled, said "No," and won. Under today's rules, if he was playing intelligently, he would have asked me to make the move, waited to see how good it was, and then intelligently accepted!

## CALLING "CHECK"

You don't have to call out "Check."

USCF rules (R) *allow* you to call check, but don't *require* it. I teach all my students not to say check. This gets some parents upset, but my reasoning is as follows: In tournament play, where all the players are experienced, it is considered somewhat insulting to call "check." It would be as if you are implying your opponent is a beginner who cannot see for himself that he is in check. Therefore, almost no good player calls check. But where does one draw the line? Do you call "Check" to players rated Under 1000 but not above? No matter how you do it, it can cause a problem. Secondly, calling "Check" to a low rated player is helping him. You wouldn't tell him that you are threatening to fork his Queen and Rook with a Knight. If he doesn't see that he is in check and touches another piece, which then has to be used to get out of check, then you are helping him learn to look to see what his opponents' moves are doing. A player

who loses because he didn't see he was in check did so because of his lack of knowledge, board vision, discipline, or whatever. In any case, each player should learn to carefully look to see what his opponent's move did, whether or not it was a check.

Calling out "Checkmate" has similar problems. Take for example two of my young students who were playing each other in a tournament. One of the players (who was otherwise losing) thought he had a checkmate and stood up and cried "Checkmate!" The other player, younger by a couple of years, felt the pressure and thus could not find either of his two legal replies, the best of which would leave him up two pieces. They asked me if it was a checkmate, but I replied that I was not allowed to help them during a tournament game. I could cite the rule for checkmate, but not tell them if a position was checkmate until the game was over *[Ed. Note: Obviously it was not therefore a checkmate, as if it had been, the game would have ended.].* Finally the younger one agreed that he was checkmated and stopped the clock. At that point I said that I was allowed to comment and that it wasn't checkmate. The result? The younger player began to cry.

I told his friend that it was a good example of why you should not call checkmate. I don't teach my students to try to intimidate their opponents into resigning. If it is a checkmate, you should just push the clock as normal and let your opponent tell you that he is mated; if it isn't checkmate, you will probably save yourself the embarrassment of calling checkmate when it is not.

### J'ADOUBE

When a piece accidently gets put somewhere other than the middle of a square, you may adjust it (R) by first saying "*J'adoube*" (French for 'I adjust') or "adjust." You may only do so on **your move,** no matter whose piece it is, and you must say so before adjusting. If you accidentally knock over a piece on the way to move another piece, as soon as you finish moving, you should say "J'adoube" and adjust the piece *before you hit the clock.* Similarly, if the piece you just moved falls over, you should adjust it before you hit the clock, if you can do so.

### ENFORCING RULES

Except for cheating that has been observed whereby the opponent would not have been able to detect it, no third party may interfere with a game (R). Therefore, besides the TD in certain situations, the only one who can enforce rules broken by your opponent is you. You have the option to call touch move, or point out any illegal moves (sometimes if it is your favor to not enforce a rule, you do not have to do so). To enforce rules is not a breach of etiquette; quite the contrary, it is expected that each player will enforce the rules and when you do so, assuming you do so politely and correctly, no opponent should be upset or ask you to excuse him. And you should not have to decide which parts of the rule book you should enforce. You should not let your opponent get away with touch move, but call an illegal move if, for example, he jumps his Bishops over pawns. You put yourself in an awkward position if you decide that you will enforce some rules but not others. Big arguments have started over players feeling that their opponents let them get away with one thing but not something else.

### INTEREFERENCE
### Third Party Interference/Observing Other Games

At kids' tournaments I sometimes see uninformed spectators think they are doing the players a favor by pointing out that a move is illegal, for example, one of the players did not move out of check. This is no favor! Such interference can have a strong effect on the outcome of the game, and is illegal. The best way to put it is: **Chess is a game between two players; besides the TD, no one else may interfere! (R)**

In the above example, the knowledge and skill of the players with regard to recognizing check and knowing what to do when there is a rules violation is part of the game. If a player loses because he does not recognize check or is unwilling to ask a TD for help, then that can work against him/her. At the start of every tournament I tell every player, "If you run into any situation for which you have a question, please stop the clock and ask me (the TD)." If they do not do so or cannot recognize a problem, it is not up to a spectator to help them. And helpful parents can be just that–helpful; that is not fair to their child's opponent, even if the interference is not for their own child's benefit. Anything which interfere's with the players (and TD's) normal enforcement of the rules creates a potential for unfairness.

Even the body language of the player's coaches or parents can have a major effect on the game. I often see a player lift a piece for a move and then look at the coach/parent for approval. Since the touch-move rule only requires them to move the piece, and not to the square they are indicating, any frown or nod of approval is really just a form of cheating, however unintentional.

There is one exception to all the above. If an opponent is cheating away from the board (so that his opponent would have no way to tell), then any third party may intervene by informing the TD if they have enough proof. For example, if a player is overheard getting advice from a coach or observed using a computer (and not just telling the coach how he is doing–it is legal to talk to your coach during a game, but I advise against it just to avoid the appearance of possibly soliciting advice), then a third party should notify the TD immediately.

## Summing It Up

Most chess games are played without any etiquette problems. Experienced players know what to expect and try to do the same. Occasionally there is a disagreement among players with the best intentions, but if everyone uses good common sense (and the

guidelines above), there are usually very few serious problems.

# 11: Illustrative Games

### Game 1:

In this game Black is a student of mine, about age 7, who has been taking lessons for a couple of months. He knows about the center and developing his pieces. He knows the value of the pieces and my number 1 guideline, "Before you move, visualize your possible moves and make sure all your pieces are safe; check to see if your opponent's pieces are safe; if not, consider taking them off." He also knows the guideline "If you see a good move, look for a better one." White is a friend of his about 9 years old. The extra age difference will about make up for the difference in knowledge, as White has never had any lessons...

|  | (400) | (500) |
|---|---|---|
| 1. | g3 | e5 |
| 2. | c4 | Nf6 |
| 3. | a3 | Nc6 |
| 4. | a4 | |

White wastes time moving a pawn twice. He does not know the guideline "Try not to move any piece twice before you move all your pieces (not pawns) once."

| 4. | ... | Bb4 |
|---|---|---|
| 5. | Ra2 | d6 |

So far, Black is following normal development guidelines and White is not, so Black has already built up a huge advantage. However, at this level this type of advantage is relatively meaningless. The player who leaves the fewest pieces *en prise* and takes off the most of his opponent's will usually win.

| 6. | g4? | Nxg4 |
|---|---|---|

When going over the game, I asked Black if he should take the g-pawn with the Knight or the Bishop. He correctly replied, "The Bishop" and, when asked why, correctly said "Because the Bishop has not moved yet." This answer, along with the fact that he took with the Knight instead, illustrates that even though beginners may know what is right, they often do not play it just because they don't take the time to think.

**7. f3??**

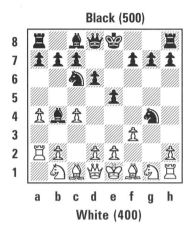

Black (500)

a b c d e f g h

White (400)

**7. ...        Nf2???**

Black sees a fork of the Rook and Queen, but overlooks several basic factors, such as that 7... Qh4 is checkmate, and that if instead 7... Nf2, the Knight can just be taken with 8. Kxf2. After the game I reminded Black to look for all checks, captures, and threats. I asked him how many checks he had. He said two. I asked him if either one was good. He replied "7... Qh4 is mate." "So why didn't you play it?" "I didn't look."

**8. Qc2??**

White also sees the fork and reasons that since his Queen is attacked, he ought to move it. This is the exact same problem as some-

one who is checked and automatically touches his King to move out of check when he could just capture the checking piece for free. The logic, "X is attacked, so I must move X" is, of course, faulty. In chess there are often better ways of protecting X (especially in beginner games!), such as removing the attacker.

**8. ...        Nxh1**
**9. Bh3??        Bxh3**
**10. Kd1??**

White does not recapture on h3 with the Knight. At this point the scoresheet became undecipherable as to the exact moves, mainly because the scorekeeper was playing Black, and for beginners it is more difficult to record algebraic notation with Black. However, what happened was that Black was winning by a large margin until he left his Queen en prise to an opposing Queen. His opponent, then up a Queen and piece for two Rooks, was unable to figure out how to win and **agreed to a draw**...

**Game 2 :**
  (500)        (1000)
**1. e4        c5**
**2. d3        d6**
**3. Bf4**

White forgets what I had suggested earlier in the day, "Knights usually develop before Bishops."

| | |
|---|---|
| **3. ...** | **Nc6** |
| **4. Nf3** | **Nf6** |
| **5. d4?** | |

White moves a pawn twice before finishing the development of his pieces. He also forgets to check to see what the pawn was doing before, which was defending his e-pawn.

| | |
|---|---|
| **5. ...** | **cxd4** |
| **6. Nbd2** | |

Now he guards his e-pawn, but at the cost of having lost his d-pawn.

| | |
|---|---|
| **6. ...** | **g6** |
| **7. e5** | **dxe5** |
| **8. Nxe5** | **Bg7** |
| **9. c4** | **dxc3 e.p.** |
| **10. bxc3** | **O-O** |

The contrast between what a 1000 player knows and what a 500 player knows is large. Black has calmly developed his pieces and castled; White has somewhat aimlessly moved a couple of pieces. But on the next move, White's game starts to fall apart badly.

**11. g4?**

This move is bad for several reasons: it does not develop a piece, it loses a pawn, and it weakens the King position. My son still sometimes makes this mistake, forgetting to ask himself, "If I make this move, where can my King go where it will be safe for the rest of the game?"

| | |
|---|---|
| **11. ...** | **Nxe5** |

Congratulations to Black for recognizing this position as a "removal of the guard" tactic. He captures the Knight which was defending the g-pawn, thus leaving the g-pawn exposed to capture next move.

| | |
|---|---|
| **12. Bxe5** | **Bxg4** |

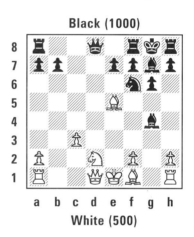

Black (1000)

White (500)

**13. Bg2??**

White doesn't see that his Queen is attacked. This goes right under the lesson about the mistaken logic "If his piece is doing one thing, it probably isn't doing another." White reasoned, "The Bishop went to g4 to take my pawn. So I know the purpose of that move. Now I can go ahead and look at what I should do." Wrong!

| | |
|---|---|
| **13. ...** | **Bxd1** |
| **14. Rxd1** | **Qa5** |

Black (1000)

White (500)

**15. B(e5!)xb7**
Illegal move!

Black now said, "That is illegal. You moved the wrong Bishop." Black then replaces his pawn on b7 and the illegally moved white Bishop is moved adjacent to c7, even though it originally came from e5! Black looked at the board, indicated the Bishop now on c7, and asked, "is that your move?" White, who was a teenager and not a youngster, was still flustered and quickly answered "Yes," even though he really had no reason to want the Bishop to be on c7.

Black (1000)

White (500)
Position after 15. B(e5!)xb7 (illegal)

Black (to move)

White (500)

**15. ...                Qxc7**

And soon thereafter **Black won easily**. After the game, I asked White "Why did you let your Bishop stay on c7 where Black could take it? After all, the touch-move rule required you to move that Bishop, but since you took your hand off of it on an illegal square (b7), you could replace

White has accidentally moved the wrong Bishop! Now he makes a big mistake. I reminded him a few times that morning, "If anything strange happens in your game, stop the clock and get the tournament director." Moving the wrong Bishop certainly qualifies as strange!

it where you came from, e5, and move it anywhere you wanted."

White replied something like "I didn't know." I said, "Then that is your fault, because I had said several times that if there is something strange going on where you don't know what the rule is, what should you do?" "Stop the clock and call the tournament director," he immediately replied. "You didn't, and you lost a piece for nothing."

### Game 3 :

| (900) | (500) |
|-------|-------|
| **1. e4** | **e5** |
| **2. Nf3** | **Nc6** |
| **3. Bb5** | **Bb4** |

Black, of course, does not know Ruy Lopez opening theory, and disregards the guideline "Knights before Bishops." Instead he mimics his higher rated opponent, but while White's Bishop move prepares castling and puts pressure on the Knight and the e5 square, Black's has no real purpose.

| **4. O-O** | **Nf6** |
|-----------|--------|
| **5. d3** | **d5??** |

Black makes several mistakes with this move. First of all, he fails to notice that by moving his d-pawn, he pins his Queen's Knight to his King (he should have asked himself, "I am planning ...d5; what is the effect of this move on my other pieces?") and

thus he will lose his e-pawn. He is also starting counter-action in the center when his opponent is castled and he is not; often a recipe for disaster.

| **6. Nxe5** | **g5?** |
|------------|--------|

Black not only does not guard his Knight on c6, which is attacked twice, but puts another pawn in take and ruins his kingside pawn field. This is one time I cannot comment on what he must have been thinking; I couldn't figure it out–I thought ...g5 was a misrecorded move, but Black said that was what he played. He also could not explain why he played ...g5.

| **7. exd5** | **O-O??** |
|------------|-----------|

Black panics and continues to follow general principles unwisely. I always tell my students that piece safcty (including King safcty) takes precedence over all other chess considerations. So, in this instance, the fact that White is attacking the black Knight with a pawn is far more important than White's need to castle early. Of course, advanced players can come up with examples where this might not be true, but 99.9% of the time giving up large amounts of material is not correct. It is important for beginners to comprehend that they should wait until they understand the game better before they start to apply the exceptions!

**8. dxc6        bxc6**
**9. Bc4        Re8?**

Black (500)

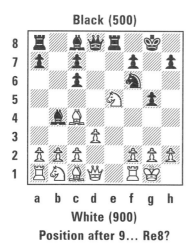

White (900)

Position after 9… Re8?

Here is another example of "Because it's forced means it can't do something else." White thought he had to move his Bishop on move 9 (although he could have captured the c-pawn with his Knight) and Black thought so, too. Thus Black did not stop to look and see that the Bishop, which had just moved to avoid capture by the pawn, also positioned himself to attack the f7 square. Of course Black is still following the general principle of "Developing all your pieces toward the center" and did not realize his f7 square is now inadequately defended.

**10. Qe1???**

White finally returns the favor and more. He also fails to see that Black's move is not much of a threat on the Knight and that he can guard his Knight by either capturing the pawn on f7 with 10. Nxf7 or capture the attacking Rook with 10. Bxf7† K moves 11. Bxe8, either way with an enormous advantage. Instead he guards his Knight by "developing" his Queen. Of course, it would have been better to choose a defense which does not lose so much material!

**10. …        Bxe1**
**11. Rxe1        Rxe5??**

Black makes yet another "Because its forced…" error. As the reader can probably tell by now, this kind of error is much more common among beginners than one might think. Black feels that since he has just captured the defender of the Knight (that is, White's Queen), he can now freely take the Knight. Black knows that a Rook is worth almost 2 pawns more than a Knight, but he didn't take the time to see that the Knight was now defended by White's recapture. Once my students eliminate this type of basic error of making quick assumptions and playing too fast, they usually get a lot better!

**12. Rxe5**

At this point Black got tired of going over this game, and I can't say I blame him! Of course, going over your games to learn about your mistakes, especially with a better player, is about the best thing you can do to improve your game. No book or computer can look at what you did and tell you the specifics of that position, along with the general principles that will help you learn. Maybe some day chess computer programs will get a lot more sophisticated! We didn't finish analyzing the game, but **White**, who first was winning easily, then losing, and now probably better (he has a Rook, a Bishop, and a pawn for the Queen, along with the Bishop pair) **won**. So even though Black won the Queen for a Bishop, it wasn't enough to overcome the large amount of skill and knowledge between a 900 player and a 500 player.

### Game 4 :

The following game segment is not spectacular, but represents several common mistakes. White, a young tournament player, is practicing against a computer. Computers are great practice opponents –they are always available, never get tired, and don't complain when they lose. Also, you can set the computer to any level you want. I always suggest that **whenever possible you should play an opponent about 200 USCF rating points above you**. This means you should win about 25% of the games. This is approximately the optimum level where your opponent is properly "pushing" you –any higher and you lose too much for it to be fun (and lose too badly for the game to be instructive)– any lower and you are not being punished enough for your mistakes. This 200 point guideline of course applies whether you are setting a computer level or trying to figure out which section of a tournament would be most beneficial.

(600)        (Computer/ "Easy")
**1. e4          Nc6**
**2. Nf3**

White has been taught to get out his Kingside pieces and castle early–but he has also been taught to set up the "little center:" d4 and e4, whenever his opponent lets him. With 1... Nc6 his opponent has allowed the little center, but White ignores his opponent and plays as if 2. d4 has been prevented.

**2. ...          Nb4**

The computer, on "Easy," violates the strong principle, "Don't move any piece in the opening twice until you move all of your pieces once, unless the move wins material or prevents the loss of material."

~113~

### 3. Bc4      b5?

And now the computer gives a free pawn. It is hard to see how a decent human could lose to a computer playing like this, but unfortunately humans have the capacity to make a large blunder that can make up for all the computer's (intentional) little blunders.

### 4. Bxb5      c6
### 5. Bc4      d5

Now Black attacks both the Bishop and the e-pawn. More experienced humans would see that the easiest solution is to first capture the pawn with 6. exd5 and then move the Bishop after the e-pawn is no longer attacked. Instead, White simply sees that his Bishop is attacked by a pawn and moves it...

### 6. Be2?      Bg4?

The computer does not capture the e-pawn, which of course is the best move. Now that his Bishop is safe, White sees that he must save the e-pawn.

### 7. exd5      Bxf3

Black voluntarily gives up the Bishop pair, which is worth almost one-half of a pawn!

### 8. Bxf3      exd5
### 9. O-O      Qd6
### 10. d4      Nxa2??

**Black (Computer/"Easy")**

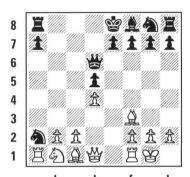

**White (600)**
**Position after 10... Nxa2?**

The computer gives away a piece in the easiest manner–moving it *right in front* of a piece that can take it for free...

### 11. Be3??

But the human does not make the capture! There are two possible explanations for this failure to take the free Knight. Either White thought that the Queen on d6 was guarding the Knight (thus misreading the diagonal force of the Queen) or he had already decided it was time to develop the Bishop and was going to do so no matter what Black moved. In either case, this is an example of why beginning humans have so much trouble–they do not carefully look at their opponent's moves and, when given some great opportunities, do not take the time to consider how they might take advantage of them.

**11. ...          Nb4**

Black gets away "Scot free."

**12. Nc3**

White is doing a commendable job of developing all his pieces. Unfortunately, he has been missing "the forest for the trees" on a number of his moves.

**12. ...          a6**

**13. Qd2          Nf6**

**14. Rad1**

White continues to blindly follow opening guidelines, such as bringing Rooks to the center. Unfortunately, since he has lost his a-pawn already, the Rook stood well on a1 and it was not beneficial to bring the Rook to the center behind the fixed d-pawns! You might call this an example of *Rote* over *Right*.

**14. ...          e6**

**15. Rfe1**

White completes his development and, with the material even, it would look to a casual observer that the game at this point has gone normally!

**15. ...          Be7**

**16. h3**

As often happens, a young player completing his development runs out of ideas. In this case he solves his problem of what to do by creating *luft* for his King.

**16. ...          a5**

**17. Ra1**

White now realizes (via Black's pawn move) that his Rook is better served on the semi-open a-file.

**17. ...          Qb6**

**18. Kh2**

But now White again decides to temporize and actually moves his King to a more vulnerable square along the open b8-h2 diagonal.

At this point **the human had to abandon the game** (dinner time?). The position, after all the earlier ups and downs, is fairly even. Let's see the same two opponents in action again:

### Game 5:

(600)          (Computer/"Easy")

**1. e4          a6**

On its easy level Black gives White the center willingly.

**2. d4**

This time White does seize the "little center."

**2. ...          d5**

**3. exd5          Qxd5**

**4. Nc3**

This time White plays the first few moves perfectly, attacking the Queen with gain of tempo. White has a comfortable advantage but, as we have seen, such a lead at this level is not necessarily likely to lead to victory!

**4. ...          Qd7**

**5. Nf3**

White correctly develops "Knights before Bishops"

**5. ...**       **Qe6†**
**6. Be2**       **b5**

Black has a mild "threat" of b4, driving the Knight away from the center. White should see this by asking himself "What can Black do to me now that he couldn't do to me before?" and get the answer 7... b4. However, there is nothing terribly wrong with White's next move.

**7. O-O**       **b4**
**8. Nb1(?)**

White avoids 8. Na4, knowing "Knight on the Rim, You're Future is Dim," except that b1 is also a rim square. Beginners tend to see the a-file and h-file as "more rim" than the first or eighth rank, but for the most part they are all rim squares. Because of the awkward placing of Black's Queen, better is 8. Na4, whereupon the Knight may soon re-enter the game via c5.

**8. ...**       **Bb7**
**9. Bd3?**

White violates the strong principle, "Don't move any piece in the opening twice until you move all of your pieces once–unless the move wins material or prevents from losing material." Except for not keeping their pieces safe, this is the most commonly violated principle by beginners.

**9. ...**       **Qc6**

Black lines up his Queen and

Bishop to aim at the g2 square on the kingside. If White doesn't pay attention to this obvious "battery," and later moves the Knight, he may find himself mated no matter how much he was winning.

**10. Bf4**       **Nd7**
**11. Nbd2**

White correctly gets all his pieces developed towards the middle and retains his slight advantage.

**11. ...**       **Qf6**
**12. g3(?)**

White sees that his Bishop on f4 is attacked, and so guards it. But there are several ways to see that a piece which is attacked is not lost:

1) Move it,
2) Guard it,
3) Put something in the way,
4) counterattack, or
5) capture the threatening piece.

Beginners often do not consider all the alternatives. Here 12. g3 is the wrong way to guard the Bishop because it weakens the white squares on the kingside, especially with the black Bishop on b7 bearing down on the long diagonal.

**12. ...**       **O-O-O**
**13. Qe2**       **Kb8**
**14. Rad1**

Just as in the previous game,

White dutifully activates his Rook by bringing it to the center. However, the Rook could have been activated closer to Black's King by playing 14. a3, threatening to capture the Black b-pawn and open up the a-file for the Rook.

**14. ...        Kc8**
**15. Rfe1      Kb8**

The "Easy" computer does not see anything constructive, and so just moves its King back and forth.

**16. Nc4**

White is making progress as his centralized pieces give him the advantage.

**16. ...        Ka7**
**17. Nh4?**

White now must move some pieces twice, but doesn't know what to do. He actually makes a move that is worse than Black's "nothing" moves of shuffling the King to and fro. Back to "Knight on the Rim..."

**17. ...        Qc6**

Black is programmed to threaten mate in ones. White sees the mate on g2, but he apparently does not see that his Knight on h4 is guarding g2. Therefore, he plays...

**18. Qf1???**

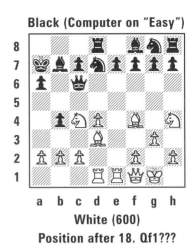

Black (Computer on "Easy")

White (600)
Position after 18. Qf1???

...instead of properly blocking the diagonal by playing something like 18. Be4, and thus does not stop the "other" mate, the one he missed:

**18. ...        Qh1#.**

Once again we see the same pattern as in the previous computer game: the human follows lots of small general principles to get an advantage, but eventually makes an enormous tactical error to throw it all away on one move. That is why chess players at the *intermediate* level can play well for 5, 10, or 20 moves in a row, but then let down their guard with one bad move and often lose, while stronger players know that if they let up their concentration on *any* move, it will likely negate all that effort they put in for all the previous moves of the game. So good players try to play their best on every move; no exceptions. Notice also that Black never moved any of his kingside pieces, yet won anyway due to White's tactical error.

**Conclusion**: Almost all beginning players make the same board vision errors. The best cure is to play as often as you can, take your time, be careful to keep your pieces safe, and learn as much as you can about all the wonderful things a chessplayer needs to know to play better, even more enjoyable games. I hope this book has taken you one large step along the way to doing so!

# About the Author

Dan Heisman started playing chess at 16 and was soon on the U.S. Chess Federation's "Top 25 Under Age 21" list.

He attended Caltech and Penn State University, receiving a Master's degree in Engineering Science.

At Penn State from 1969-1971 he was the captain and first board for the varsity chess team under coach IM Donald Byrne.

In 1972 he teamed with Byrne and Penn State players to win the U.S. Team Championship.

In 1973 Heisman won the Philadelphia Closed Invitational Championship ahead of (now) IM Tim Taylor, Boris Baczynsky, and others.

In 1977 he won the Philadelphia Open Championship. At the time of this writing Heisman's FIDE rating was 2285.

Since college he has played infrequently, preferring to spend his chess time writing and teaching. Heisman was an active tournament director during the 1970's and served as President of the *Chaturanga Chess Club* in PA. He has given simultaneous exhibitions and taught chess to many groups; he currently serves as coordinator for the *Huntingdon Valley Chess Society Juniors*, a club open to any junior player.

Among his chess students are Danny Benjamin, who achieved a national master's ranking at age 13, Steven Kendrex, the 1993-1994 National Kindergarten Champion, and Matthew Traldi, who became a master at 12 and was the 1997-98 US co-7th Grade Champion.

He is a full-time chess instructor and founder of *Heisman's Chess Trophies Instructional Club*. He also works with the Philadelphia branch of the program, which teaches chess at inner-city schools. Heisman has written two other chess books and many articles for various magazines, including *Chess Life*. In 1979, Heisman was voted "The Outstanding Local Chess Columnist" by the Chess Journalists of America for his articles in the Bucks County (PA) *Courier Times*.

He became the first author to write an extensive article about his experience in a man-machine collaboration experiment in postal chess. Heisman is a member of the International Computer Chess Association, and in that capacity worked at both of the *Kasparov vs. Deep Blue* matches, appearing on *Good Morning America*, *CNN*, and network television, as well as being quoted in the *New York Times*. Heisman currently lives with his son Delen, and wife Shelly, in Wynnewood, Pennsylvania.

STOP

# INDEX

70, 73, 98, 104

## V
value (pieces)   21, 50, 54
variation(s)   53, 95
video (tapes)   26, 46
violation   99
visual aids   35
visualize   8, 90, 107
vulnerab(e, ility)   62

## W
waste time   58-59
weak opponents/players   51, 56, 62
weak pawn   56
weakened squares   62
weaker opponent(s)/player(s)   53, 61,
   88, 101
weakness(es)   62, 87
weighted   73
winning by a pawn   61
wooden sets   73
work   76
worried   20-21

## X
x-rays   19, 57

## Y
young player   79
youngster(s)   42, 67, 88
youthful ego   18

# Colophon

*Everyone's Second Chess Book* was typeset in Times 12/14. The diagram font is Thinkers' Press, Inc.'s *C.R. Horowitz.*

Cover Design: Bass Long
Editing and Layout: Bob Long
Interior Art and Photos: Bass Long
Proofing: Dan Heisman & Bob Long

We want to thank the kids who took a 6-week brush up chess course at the Bettendorf Public Library for allowing their pictures to be taken.

Requests for permissions and republication rights should be submitted in writing (not e-mail) to:
Editor in Chief
Thinkers' Press, Inc.
P.O. Box 8
Davenport, IA 52805-0008
USA

Other matters:
e-mail: blong@chessco.com

For information on the U.S. Chess Federation write:
3054 Route 9W
New Windsor, NY 12553

**Contents of ACTION CHESS**

Some years back when C.J.S. Purdy was publishing his *Chess World* magazine he had written a series of articles on how to learn a "system" of openings which wouldn't require as much memorization as many openings do. He called it his *All Purpose System/Defense* (APS/APD). The openings also had a certain amount of "safety" built into them (except perhaps for his recommendation of the Sicilian Dragon as an alternative to his recommended French Burn Variation).

As researcher and proofer NY Master Ron Weick discovered these openings also had the advantage of material (good material!) he hadn't seen anywhere else. Purdy's son-in-law Frank Hutchings (and his sparring partner on many occasions) said Purdy kept constantly up-to-date, even in his later years, with respect to opening theory.

We changed his "Ten Hour Course" to "24 Hours" because we assembled a little extra material and added many notes to bring his writings current with theory. We also know people today are even busier than they were in CJS's time. Try it!

Available from:
**Chessco • P.O. Box 8 • Davenport, IA 52805-0008**
or by calling: 1-800-397-7117
Please add $3 for S&H.
Chessco is a subsidiary of Thinkers' Press, Inc.